Holy Grail

Connecting the Holy Grail to Atlantis

(The Holy Grail for a Balanced and Harmonious Life)

Betty Langley

Published By **Bella Frost**

Betty Langley

All Rights Reserved

Holy Grail: Connecting the Holy Grail to Atlantis (The Holy Grail for a Balanced and Harmonious Life)

ISBN 978-1-77485-614-7

No part of this guidebook shall be reproduced in any form without permission in writing from the publisher except in the case of brief quotations embodied in critical articles or reviews.

Legal & Disclaimer

The information contained in this ebook is not designed to replace or take the place of any form of medicine or professional medical advice. The information in this ebook has been provided for educational & entertainment purposes only.

The information contained in this book has been compiled from sources deemed reliable, and it is accurate to the best of the Author's knowledge; however, the Author cannot guarantee its accuracy and validity and cannot be held liable for any errors or omissions. Changes are periodically made to this book. You must consult your doctor or get professional medical advice before using any of the suggested remedies, techniques, or information in this book.

Upon using the information contained in this book, you agree to hold harmless the Author from and against any damages, costs, and expenses, including any legal fees potentially resulting from the application of any of the information provided by this guide. This disclaimer applies to any damages or injury caused by the use and application, whether directly or indirectly, of any advice or information presented, whether for breach of contract, tort, negligence, personal injury, criminal intent, or under any other cause of action.

You agree to accept all risks of using the information presented inside this book. You need to consult a professional medical practitioner in order to ensure you are both able and healthy enough to participate in this program.

TABLE OF CONTENTS

Chapter 1: Holy Grail 1

Chapter 2: The Holy Grail And King Arthur 20

Chapter 3: Conspiracy Theories And The Location Of The Holy Grail Today 39

Chapter 4: The Grail Christianized 61

Chapter 5: Grail Quests 75

Chapter 6: The Gnostic Grail 96

Chapter 7: The Templars Grail 117

Chapter 8: Symbolism Of The Grail 135

Chapter 9: The Quest Continues 158

Chapter 10: The Grail Today 174

Chapter 1: Holy Grail

The term 'Holy Grail' is commonly used to describe something that is out of reach, difficult or impossible to obtain, an object or goal sought after due to its great significance. But it is based on something that many people believe is real, while others think it no longer exists and yet more are of the opinion that it is a fictitious item that only existed in people's imagination.

To the true believers, the Holy Grail is something that has miraculous powers and which has been sought after for many centuries with no positive outcome. Numerous tales have been told about the quest for the Holy Grail and its fascination lives on to this day, largely due to the mystery that surrounds it and the dearth of information that ensures its location, if there is one, remains unidentified.

The legend of the Holy Grail has grown over the centuries, starting with the death of Jesus, enhanced by the Arthurian legends of the Middle Ages and reinforced by modern culture that includes films and novels. It is a story of magical powers, heroic quests and, ultimately, failure due to the continuing lack of knowledge about the Holy Grail's whereabouts.

The Holy Grail is thought by many to be the most holy of all artefacts for Christians and it remains a priceless yet elusive relic. The quest for it is considered to be one of the great adventures although few get to undertake it and, as yet, none have been truly successful.

What the Holy Grail is Supposed To Be

Depending on your point of view, the Holy Grail is either a mythical object that never existed or was an actual item that may or may not still exist today. The most generally accepted definition is that it is a dish, cup or plate that was used by Jesus to provide food for his disciples during the Last Supper before his death.

Due to its significance, the Holy Grail is mentioned several times in the Bible, describing Jesus' last meal with his apostles when he shared bread and wine with them. In Luke 22.20, Jesus says: "This cup is God's new covenant sealed with my blood, which is poured out to you."

There are similar mentions in Matthew 26.26-29 and Mark 14.22-26. The new covenant represented the teaching of Jesus and allowed the apostles to live in heaven after their death. The cup is not mentioned again in the Bible after the Last Supper.

An alternative version of the cup's significance is that it was used by Joseph of Arimathea to catch Jesus' blood, which flowed from a wound in his side that resulted from it being pierced by a Roman soldier's spear. Although there is an account of Jesus' death in John 19.31-37, the use of the cup to collect the blood is not mentioned.

Joseph of Arimathea is, however, included in subsequent text (John 19.38-42) that describes the burial of Jesus. Joseph was rich and a member of the council that had interrogated Jesus, although he did not approve of the other members' actions but was unable to do anything to prevent them. He was, by some accounts, Jesus' great uncle.

Pilate apparently gave Joseph permission to take Jesus' body away for burial. Assisted by Nicodemus, a Jewish leader among the Pharisees, he prepared and wrapped Jesus' body in accordance with Jewish burial custom. The body was placed in a tomb, now known as the Holy Sepulchre, which was closed off with a large stone. The tomb and the crucifixion site, which were adjacent, are now enclosed by a large church to mark the most holy of all Christian sites.

By one account, Joseph was subsequently imprisoned in a rock tomb and was left to starve. He was, however, visited by Jesus, who explained to him the mysteries of the cup, and was then sustained by the Holy Grail, which provided food and drink every day. This was the first recorded incidence of the Grail's magical powers, which grew over the years.

After escaping from the tomb many years later, Joseph apparently travelled to Britain, taking the Holy Grail with him to Glastonbury and founding a dynasty of Grail keepers that would eventually include Perceval. In other accounts, Alain, one of Joseph's relatives, carried the Grail to Britain. Glastonbury is one of the supposed locations of the relic today although other accounts, particularly the Arthurian legends, report that the Grail was taken to a spectacular castle at Corbenic where it was guarded by the Grail Kings.

Guardians of the Holy Grail

Various books suggest the secret of the Holy Grail was known to only a select few, including the Knights Templar, the Cathars and the Priory of Sion, a secret society.

The Cathars were a religious group that rejected all ideas of priesthood and the use of church buildings. This put them at odds with the Roman Catholic Church, especially since many of their other beliefs were exactly the opposite of those put forward by Rome.

The Cathars' ideas are thought to come from Persia or the Byzantine Empire, although they and their religion flourished in the Languedoc area, bordered by the Mediterranean, the Pyrenees and the rivers Garonne, Tam and Rhône. The religion gained popularity, much to the annoyance of the Roman Catholic Church, which was ridiculed and criticized by Cathar supporters.

This led to the Albigension Crusade on the orders of Pope Innocent III and the war against the Cathars lasted two generations. A war of terror ensued from 1208, resulting in an estimated 50,000 men, women and children being killed.

The first papal Inquisition was established to erase any lasting resistance and the last vestiges of Catharism were wiped out by the end of the Fourteenth Century. A significant episode in this campaign, particularly as it affected the Holy Grail, was the nine-month siege of Montsegur in 1243 by papal forces amounting to 10,000 armed troops.

When the Cathars were besieged, they had already evacuated their material treasures. However, on the night before they surrendered and 210 believers were burned to death, certain other items were removed from Montsegur and their identity remains a mystery. It may have been books or manuscripts but there is speculation that the Holy Grail was among the items.

In various books, most recently The Da Vinci Code, the theory put forward is that the Holy Grail is not a material object but represents the royal blood of Jesus that is carried down through his descendants, who founded the Merovingian dynasty of France. The Priory of Sion was supposedly established in 1099 to restore the royal line with the help of the Knights Templar, an organization which it had helped to establish.

The Priory of Sion aimed to do this restoring the Merovingian dynasty to power, protecting royal claimants, establishing a new order through a Holy European Empire and creating a Masonic state religion. The Roman Catholic Church supposedly countered these aims by trying to kill off all Jesus' descendants and their guardians — the Cathars and the Knights Templar.

This story of the Priory of Sion is considered by many to be total fiction, the real organization of that name being established in 1956 to defend council tenants. Its founder, however, built up the aura surrounding the Priory of Sion by creating false parchments that linked him to the French throne.

This claim was later admitted to be a fraud but the tale took on a new lease of life with the publication of Holy Blood Holy Grail in 1982, which brought up the theory of the Grail representing Jesus' blood line. It was given a further boost by repeated mention of the Priory of Sion in The Da Vince Code. As a result, several organizations now claim to be the Priory of Sion.

Origins of the Term

Like many historical terms, the origin of Holy Grail has several variations. 'Grail' is generally thought to come from the Latin word gradale, meaning a dish that was brought to the table during the different grades or stages of a meal. The word is also sometimes thought to originate from the Old French word grail, generally meaning a cup or bowl made from earth, wood or metal.

Some late medieval writers referred to the Old French term san graal or san greal, which translates as 'Holy Grail'. A variation of this is sung real, which means royal blood. Some theorists have used this interpretation to imply that the Grail is really a symbol of Jesus' own blood line.

This theory has been explored in several books, most famously The Da Vinci Code, which outlined how Jesus had lived on, married Mary Magdalene, and their descendants are alive today. An earlier publication, Holy Blood, Holy Grail, also explored the theory and portrayed the Grail as being symbolic of Mary Magdalene as the receptacle of Jesus' blood line.

If there is any truth in this latter theory, the supposition is that the Roman Catholic Church tried to kill off all those descendants using the Crusades and the Inquisition in order to maintain its power.

Powers and Features Attributed to The Holy Grail

The Holy Grail's supposed magical properties, which first surfaced with its ability to sustain Joseph of Arimathea in his rock tomb, are thought to be based on the magic cauldrons of Celtic mythology. The Cauldrons of Dragda of Irish myth told the tale of a large wheeled vessel that had magical properties.

Always full of food, it could satisfy someone's hunger, renew strength and heal a person. Celtic cauldrons were used in ceremonial feasting and ritual examples have been found in Wales, indicating their religious importance. Perhaps the best known, found in the peat bogs of Denmark, is the Gunderstrup Cauldron that could hold up to 28.5 gallons of liquid.

The Cauldron of Ceridwen, a Celtic goddess who inhabited the Otherworld, inspired the common image of witches stirring a cauldron. The Celtic warrior god Bran obtained his magic cauldron from the goddess and it was capable of restoring life to dead warriors.

Various Welsh myths also tell of a magic cauldron that sometimes brings the dead back to life. Such tales fit in with the theory that the Grail derives from early Celtic folklore, although many others think it is a purely Christian symbol.

The belief in its Celtic origins aligns with many Celtic tales, where a common theme was the need to ask the right question or find the correct solution. In Chrétien's Perceval, the hero was supposed to ask a question— 'What rich man was served from the grail?' or 'Why did that drop of blood flow from the white shaft?' — In order to heal the Fisher King and restore the wasted lands, but failed to do so. In De Boron's Perceval, on his second visit to the castle, Perceval's question was 'Sire, by the faith that you owe to me and that you owe to all men, tell me what one serves with these things that I see borne here?'

Christian Origins

The earliest stories do portray the Grail in a Christian manner and it is thought they were written to promote the Roman Catholic sacrament of the Holy Communion. In addition, Grail imagery has been found in Twelfth Century wall paintings in the Museu Nacional d'Art de Catalunya in Barcelona.

These paintings were originally in various churches in the Catalan Pyrenees and show iconic images of the Virgin Mary holding a bowl that radiates fire. The paintings are dated prior to Chrétien de Troyes' writings and could be the inspiration for the legend of the Holy Grail.

The consensus now is that, although the central theme of the Grail is Christian, the settings and imagery are drawn from Celtic material. Due to the Grail's pagan origins, however, the authorities of the Roman Catholic Church were never able to fully accept the story. The supposedly magical restorative powers that it possessed are at odds with Christian teachings.

Controversy still reigns, nonetheless, as to what the grail actually is, with some arguing that it represents a series of symbols and another theory being that it refers to the Shroud of Turin. There are also beliefs that the legend of the Grail connects to a renewal of the traditional sacrament of the Eucharist in medieval times.

Mentions of the Holy Grail in Literature

Although the Holy Grail is associated with the last days of Jesus, there is little or no mention of it in literature until the Middle Ages. That does rather reinforce some people's views that it is a fictitious object that was invented for the sole purpose of telling romantic tales.

The Middle Ages was a romantic era that was full of stories of forbidden love that people were willing to die for. It was an age of gallantry and chivalry, of heroic deeds. And no deed was more heroic than the quest for the Holy Grail.

Most of the Grail romances were written between the years 1180 and 1240. Many of them are in French but there are versions in other languages that include English and German, although some of these are simply translations from the French originals. After the end of the Thirteenth Century, there was little further mention of the legend of the Holy Grail until recent times.

Early mentions of the Grail

The first such mention of the Holy Grail was in 1180, in Perceval, le Conte du Graal (The History of the Grail), a romance written by French poet Chrétien de Troyes, which was one of a series of five Arthurian romances that he wrote. It was based on a source given to him by Count Philip of Flanders, who was his patron. It was never finished due to

Chrétien's untimely death but was a huge work comprising around 60,000 verses.

This tale diverged from earlier stores about King Arthur that had few adventures involving his knights; here, the power of the knights was increasing as that of monarchs reduced. In the story, a Welsh youth named Perceval saw the Grail, which was a platter or dish, as part of a wondrous procession that also included a blood-stained lance (possibly the one used to pierce Jesus' side) and candelabras. The Grail contained a holy host that was able to sustain life and lit up the room.

Perceval was a simpleton who eventually became a knight and, through his association with the Grail, was able to achieve great things. Although this story was independent of other tales, it is part of the Arthurian legends and there are later links to King Arthur's knights.

Chrétien made no connection between Jesus and the Grail and actually referred to the object as 'a grail', indicating that he simply perceived it as a dish or bowl rather than something that had special significance. Such a dish would be used to serve various foods but here it contained only a single communion wafer that would provide sustenance for the crippled father of the Fisher King. In this respect, it is often thought that Chrétien meant the wafer to have significance in the story rather than the cup that contained it.

Since the story remained unfinished, others tried to complete it for him in works that were known as the Grail Continuations. One of these writers was another French poet, Robert de Boron, who wrote three books that referred to the Holy Grail. In fact, whereas Chrétien had referred to 'a grail', de Boron was the first writer to describe it as the Holy Grail and put it in a more Christian context.

The first of these, Joseph d'Arimathea, described how the cup was used at the Last Supper and also to catch the blood of Jesus after his crucifixion. This latter event is not mentioned in the Bible and is thought to be a fictional element in the book.

Boron then relates how the Grail was brought to Britain by someone known as the Rich Fisher, rather than by Joseph as in other stories. His second book, Merlin, covers the creation of the Round Table and the tale of King Arthur.

The third book, Perceval, was lost but a separate version of this was featured in the Didcot Perceval, thought to be a prose adaptation of Perceval and named after its former owner. This version purportedly told the tale of Perceval's quest for the Grail and how he became its guardian. It differs from other stories that credit Gawain (in the German story Diu Crône — The Crown) or Galahad as the finders of the Grail.

Different Versions of The Grail Story

Parzival, written in 1210 by Wolfram von Eschenbach, was a long poem that ran to sixteen books. It stated that the Grail was a stone that fell from the sky. This stone, known as lapsit exillis (the Philosopher's Stone), was sustained by a consecrated Host and it is believed the author based his idea on the Muslim Kaaba, the stone at Mecca that was brought from heaven. Its essence was so pure that it was able to nourish someone who was in its presence as well as slowing ageing and sustaining a mortally wounded person.

The first guardians of this magical stone were supposedly angels who had remained neutral during Lucifer's rebellion. They brought it down to earth where it was kept at Munsalvaesche, the castle of the first Grail King Titurel, where it was nourished by its food-giving power.

In Le Haut Livre du Graal, or Perlesvaus, published around 1212, the Grail and the bleeding lance disappeared with the death of the Fisher King and the quest this time was for a gold circlet, known as the Circle of Gold. This represented the crown of thorns that was put on Jesus' head. The other holy relics, including the Grail, reappeared on the death of Perceval's wicked uncle.

Other publications include Welsh folk tale Mabinogion, in which parallels can be drawn between the tale of Bran the Blessed and his life restoring cauldron, and the Fisher King and the Grail in other stories. In fact, Bran the Blessed was sometimes referred to as the 'Pierced Thighs' since he had similar wounds to those that had been inflicted on the Fisher King. This gives rise to the belief that Bran was the origin of the Fisher King.

In Peredur son of Efrawg, there was no Grail as such and in its place was a platter that contained the severed head of the hero's kinsman. There was also the French prose romance Grand St. Graal, where Christ presented a book of his history to a pious hermit, and three French romances that portrayed the history of the Grail and the subsequent quest for it.

The Vulgate Cycle, believed to have been compiled by Cistercian monks and published between 1225 and 1237, treated the Grail as a symbol of divine grace. It dealt with Lancelot's love for Queen Guinevere and described how Galahad, the illegitimate son of Lancelot and Elaine, carried out a quest for the Grail.

By now, the search for the Holy Grail was no longer a quest of chivalry but had become a spiritual quest. The emphasis was largely on the hero, who had to be pure of spirit and even had to be a monk as well as a knight.

The Grail stories from the Middle Ages split into two groups. The first group covered the period when Joseph of Arimathea acquired and guarded the Grail while the second group dealt with the knights of King Arthur and their quest for the Holy Grail.

Common among many of the tales was the theme of a simpleton who achieves by guileless means what many wise men are incapable of doing. In his ignorance, he fails in his quest initially but eventually, through learning and experience, he attains his aims.

Later Grail stories

Sir Thomas Mallory's Le Morte d'Arthur, which is still well-known today, continued the story in the Fifteenth Century. After a long period when little was mentioned of the Holy Grail, Alfred Lord Tennyson revived the interest in the Nineteenth Century with Idylls of the King, an Arthurian cycle.

Twentieth Century Italian philosopher Julius Evola believed the Holy Grail was 'a symbolic expression of hope and of the will of specific ruling classes in the Middle Ages, who wanted to reorganize and reunite the entire Western world as it was at that time into a Holy Empire based on a transcendental, spiritual basis'. The Sign of the Seal by Graham Hancock proposed that the story of the Grail is actually a coded description of the stone tablets that were stored in the Ark of the Covenant.

Several paintings featuring the Holy Grail appeared at various times, including The Damsel of the Sanct Grael by Dante Gabriel

Rossetti, which featured a woman holding the Grail in one hand. In the early Twentieth Century, Edwin Austin Abbey produced for the Boston Public Library a mural series that depicted the Quest for the Holy Grail.

Belgian artist Francoise Taylor created a series of eighteen engravings in 1948. These provided illustrations from Mallory's Le Morte d'Arthur and included two pictures that featured the Grail — The Sangreal and The Quest of the Sangreal.

More recently, most writings about the Holy Grail have been works of fiction that have based their stories on authentic events in early literature but have elaborated and added to these writings and put them in a modern day context.

Chapter 2: The Holy Grail And King Arthur

Most stories from the Middle Ages about the Holy Grail were romantic tales of gallantry and chivalry. The most gallant of these were the tales of King Arthur and his knights and their quest for the Grail. At that time, the quest for the Holy Grail was considered the highest spiritual pursuit that a knight could undertake.

After the Holy Grail was brought to Britain, supposedly by Joseph of Arimathea although various others are credited with this task, some accounts have it being kept in a mysterious and spectacular castle, known as Corbenic. Here, the Grail was guarded by the Grail Kings, who were reported to be the descendants of Joseph's daughter Anna and her husband Brons.

The Grail at Corbenic Castle

The Corbenic name has had many interpretations over the years. The most likely of these is that it originates from Corbin-Vicus, effectively meaning the settlement of the crow or raven from a combination of French and Latin words.

There is also a view that it translates as 'Bran's Settlement', Bran or Brons being having been Joseph's son-in-law and one of the earliest Grail Kings. Other explanations are that the name derives from the Old Welsh Cors, referring to the Horn of Plenty as the Holy Grail was sometimes known, or the Old French Corps-Benoit that means 'Holy Body' or the Body of Christ.

Corbenic Castle was reputed to be a magical place where the normal rules of the human world did not apply. Few mortals would be allowed in and, of those that were, most would later be unable to re-enter or even find the castle again. Several searched in vain for many years to locate Corbenic Castle and only the privileged few were eventually successful.

There was also a view that the castle could appear in different places and those who were able to find it must pass some sort of initiation first before they were allowed entry. This may be in the form of a series of tests that make up the quest for the Grail.

After several centuries, the location of Corbenic Castle was forgotten but the prophesy at the Court of King Arthur was that it would eventually be discovered by a descendant of Joseph of Arimathea. That man would be the best knight in the land.

Perceval and the Celtic myths

Pre-dating King Arthur's knights was the tale of Perceval, told by Robert de Boron, who was the first Grail hero and its last guardian. At the time Perceval discovered the castle, it was guarded by the Fisher King, who was apparently Perceval's grandfather, Bron, the brother-in-law of Joseph of Arimathea, and land around it was laid waste.

Perceval dined at Corbenic Castle and saw a wondrous procession that involved youths passing before him carrying magnificent objects. These included a bleeding lance, candelabras and the elaborately decorated Grail.

Depending on the version of the story you read, the lance had been used to cripple either the Fisher King or his father, by piercing both his thighs. Other tales have the Fisher King as the Maimed King, while some describe them as being different people, which all adds to the confusion and mystery that surrounds the Grail. Perceval could apparently have cured him of his wounds if he had asked the correct questions, but did not do so because he had been told not to talk too much and so remained silent throughout the meal.

The wounding of the Fisher King was supposedly carried out by an angel wielding the lance. This was apparently the fate of many who slept in the same chamber as the Grail, with death being the eventual outcome from what was known as the Dolorous Stroke and only the knight Gawain surviving the wound. That was due to Elaine, the daughter of Pelles, an early Grail King, using the Grail to heal him.

A common theme among Celtic myths was that, when a king became ill, the land he ruled over also became barren. That was because a king was considered to be wedded to the land over which he ruled and so the health of the king was inextricably bound to that of the land.

Perceval supposedly failed in his early quest to obtain the Holy Grail because he wasn't sufficiently mature. He had to grow both spiritually and mentally before he was able to find the Grail again.

The original Perceval tale was told by Chrétien de Troyes but was never finished. It is widely thought that Chrétien meant to describe

Perceval's second visit to the castle, when he would ask the appropriate questions and achieve the quest, but he died before he was able to do so.

The failure of Perceval to ultimately complete the quest left the way open for others to be more successful. This was the start of the Arthurian legends, which began when Merlin created the Round Table and Arthur was able to pull the sword from the rock to prove that he was worthy to be the King of Britain and successor to Uther.

The Importance of Swords in The Arthurian Legends

The sword was the most significant weapon at the time of King Arthur and appeared prominently in many Arthurian legends. Often, the sword had symbolic and noble meaning, and the wielding of a particular sword was necessary to solve the mystery of the Grail.

Certain of the Grail stories tell of a beautiful sword that was given to Perceval by the Fisher King but which broke when used. The sword could only be repaired by the Grail hero, who by so doing would understand the secrets of the Grail. Gawain visited Corbenic

Castle twice but was unable to fix the sword and so failed in the quest.

Galahad was the illegitimate son of Lancelot and Elaine, born after Elaine tricked Lancelot into sleeping with her by making him think he was sleeping with Guinevere. Thus, she became the mother of the greatest Grail knight, who successfully restored the sword.

Another version of the sword story covers one with strange straps, which would be awarded to the knight who rescued a maiden from the besieged castle of Montesclere. The successful knight would be the greatest knight in the world and, although the story is unfinished, either Perceval or Gawain was thought to be the successful knight.

An alternative version has the hero as Galahad, who found the sword on a magical ship. An inscription on the hilt stated that the Chosen One would be able to wield it, and only Galahad was able to grip the handle properly.

The most famous Arthurian sword story, of course, is that of the sword in the stone. This sword came floating down the river to Camelot, fast in a large block of marble, having apparently been placed there by

Merlin. An inscription on the sword's pommel stated that only the best knight could draw it from the stone.

Lancelot would not touch the sword so Arthur ordered Gawain to try, but he failed to move the sword. Galahad, however, was successful and later used the sword to wound Gawain. His success in drawing the sword marked him as the greatest knight, even better than his father, and ultimately destined to complete the Grail quest.

The Quest for the Grail by King Arthur's Knights

Although the location of the castle of Corbenic had been long forgotten by the time of King Arthur, the prophesy at his court was that it would be rediscovered. This achievement would fall to a descendent of Joseph of Arimathea and he would be the best knight in the land.

The successful knight would be the only one who could sit in the Siege Perilous (or the Perilous Seat). It had been reserved by Merlin for the knight who would be successful in the quest for the Holy Grail.

This was a vacant seat at the Round Table and was the thirteenth seat, symbolizing Judas' place at the Last Supper. Anyone who sat in it other than the successful knight would supposedly die as a result.

The search for the Grail began with a brief vision of it when it appeared before the assembled Knights of the Round Table. It was seen by them as a dazzling and profound vision of light that filled each one of them with wisdom and generosity, and they were all struck dumb by its beauty. The Grail filled the hall with delicious odors and the knights feasted and drank better than they had ever done before.

This coincided with the arrival of Galahad, who appeared to have the necessary attributes and sat in the Siege Perilous, the previously empty seat that was reserved for the knight who could complete the quest for the Holy Grail. It was the principal quest of King Arthur's knights.

The successful completion of this quest would supposedly heal the Fisher King's wounds, renew the wasted lands that surrounded Corbenic Castle and also fulfil the knights who were able to find the Grail. However, King Arthur was not overly keen on his knights undertaking the quest for he feared many of them may perish in the attempt, which did prove to be the case.

The quest took many years, with Arthur's knights covering various parts of Britain in their search. In one version of the story, Preiddeu Annwfn (Spoils of the Otherworld), Arthur set out with his knights to the Celtic Otherworld where they intended to capture the Cauldron of Annwfn. They eventually found it at a castle of glass on an island but were unable to overcome the ensuing perils and only seven men returned home.

In another version, they finally found the castle and, after Perceval failed because he was not pure enough and left empty handed, Lancelot was unable to gain entry due to him being an adulterer. Galahad, however, was the most chaste and so was admitted. He was able to view the cup, which resulted in the completion of the quest, the healing of the crippled king and the barren lands becoming fertile again, as well as bringing fulfilment to his life.

Other versions of the story have Sir Bors added as another knight involved in the quest. This was intended to show a different type of chastity — faithfulness within marriage.

The Crusades and the Knights Templar

There were a total of eight major Crusades, which occurred between 1096 and 1291, and they were basically a series of religious wars between Christians and Muslims. They were intended to demonstrate the superior power of Western Europe over the Islamic Empire of the Middle East and North Africa, which was a major power at the time, as well as securing control of various holy sites that each of the groups considered sacred.

The Beginning of The Crusades

The First Crusade took place between 1096 and 1099, and was in response to a request to Pope Urban II by Alexius I, who had seized the Byzantine throne in 1081. The Byzantine Empire formed the western half of what had been the Roman Empire and had more power than Western Europe. However, considerable territory had been lost to the invading Turks and Alexius requested mercenary Western troops to help repel the threat.

Relations between Christians in the east and the west were improving at the time so the Pope called on Western Christians to help recapture the Holy Lands from the Muslims. A tremendous response saw ordinary citizens and members of the military join the armed pilgrimage wearing the cross as a Christian symbol. Various knightly military orders, including the Knights Templar, the Hospitallers and the Teutonic Knights, joined the Crusade to defend the Holy Land and protect pilgrims travelling there.

Four armies were formed of troops from different parts of Western Europe. They left for Byzantium in August 1096 but were preceded by a less-organized band that was known as the 'Peoples' Crusade' and was led by a preacher called Peter the Hermit. This force was crushed by the Turks at Cibotus after crossing the Bosporus despite being advised to wait for the main force.

A separate Crusader group attracted widespread criticism when it massacred Jews in various Rhineland towns, causing a major crisis in relations between Jews and Christians.

The four main armies captured Nicea in Anatolia in June 1097, followed by Antioch in June 1098. They had earlier been asked to swear an oath of allegiance to Alexius and to grant him authority over any captured land but only one of the groups agreed to this. As a result, relations between them deteriorated, although the combined forces continued to advance through Anatolia.

After these early successes, many Crusaders left for home. The conquered territory was divided into four Crusader states with settlements in Jerusalem, Elesse, Antioch and Tripoli. They were guarded by formidable castles but Muslim forces waged a jihad (holy war) and recaptured some of the territory, culminating in the fall of Edessa and the loss of the northernmost of the four Crusader states.

Further Crusades

This loss prompted the start of the Second Crusade, beginning in 1147. The largest ever Crusader army, some 50,000 troops, attacked the Syrian stronghold of Damascus after an earlier defeat at Dorylaeum. This culminated in a humiliating defeat for the Crusaders and brought an ignominious end to the Second Crusade.

Muslim forces seized Cairo in 1169, forcing the Crusader army to evacuate, having failed several times to capture Egypt. A major campaign against Jerusalem by Saladin ended with the loss of the city and surrounding territory as well as the virtual destruction of the Christian army at Hattin in 1187.

These losses led to the launch of the Third Crusade under the leadership of the Emperor Barbarossa, King Philip II of France and England's King Richard I (or Richard the Lionheart). Barbarossa was drowned at Anatolia, before his army reached Syria, but King Richard's forces defeated Saladin at Arsuf in the only real battle of this Crusade, re-establishing control of part of the region. The Crusade ended with the signing of a peace treaty that recreated the Kingdom of Jerusalem.

A Fourth Crusade was requested in 1198 by Pope Innocent III but the Crusaders diverted the mission to defeat Alexius III, the current Byzantine emperor. His nephew succeeded him as Alexius IV but was killed in a palace coup in 1204 after he attempted to submit the Byzantine church to Rome. As a result, the Crusaders declared war on Constantinople, leading to its fall and near destruction, and the end of the Fourth Crusade.

The last of the Crusades

A further four Crusades followed in the years 1208-1271. Added to these was a so-called Children's Crusade in 1212, comprising thousands of children who vowed to march to Jerusalem but never made it, and the Albigension Crusade from 1208 to 1229 in France as well as the Baltic Crusades of 1211-1225 in Transylvania. The aim of the main Crusades was to combat anyone and anything that was perceived to be an enemy of the Christian faith.

The Fifth Crusade attacked Egypt in 1221 but was forced to surrender to Muslin defenders. The Sixth Crusade in 1229 achieved the negotiated transfer of Jerusalem to Crusader control although Muslims regained control ten years later when the peace treaty expired.

Louis IX of France organised the Seventh Crusade, against Egypt, from 1248 to 1254, although this ended in failure. The Eighth Crusade was launched in 1270 by Louis IX in response to the demolition of Antioch by the

Mamluks, who had taken power in Egypt. He aimed to protect the remaining Crusader states in Syria but Louis died after the mission was redirected to Tunis.

The last Crusade, sometimes known as the Ninth Crusade but more generally grouped with the Eighth that had not completed, was led by Edward I of England. It achieved little and one of the last remaining Crusader cities, Acre, fell to the Mamluks in 1291, marking the end of the Crusades and the states they had established.

Minor Crusades were subsequently organized but had little support. These were mainly aimed at conquering non-Christian regions or removing Muslims from territories they had captured. They continued after 1291 right through to the Sixteenth Century but any support they had ran out as papal authority declined during the Reformation.

Although the Crusades did eventually lead to defeat for the Christian forces, they did increase the wealth of the Roman Catholic Church and the power of the Pope. They also increased Western and Christian influence, improved trade, created more demand for goods that were required for the wars and increased interest in travel and learning that many think helped bring the Renaissance into being.

The Crusades did, however, cause much resentment among Muslims, who regarded the Crusaders as immoral savages who caused great suffering to non-Christians. Some of that resentment is still apparent today and perhaps is the cause of many of our present troubles.

The Role of The Knights Templar

The Knights Templar's involvement in the Crusades and ownership of the Holy Grail largely centered around the First Crusade. The Templars were reputed to have returned to Britain with many well-known Biblical relics that they had obtained, among them the Holy Grail. Some of these relics were supposedly hidden in various places throughout the British Isles.

By some accounts, after the Holy Grail was found in the Holy Land, it was initially owned by Prince Raymond of Antioch. He gave it, in 1149, to his niece, Eleanor of Aquitaine, who took it to England and married Henry II. The cup was guarded by the Knights Templar, who were at the height of their power in the

Twelfth and Thirteenth Centuries. By 1280, however, their influence was in decline and the fate of the Holy Grail from then forward is less clear.

One story recounts that nine Knights Templar discovered the Holy Grail buried near Solomon's Temple, in the remains of a cell where Jesus had been held. They used their knowledge of its presence to persuade the Pope to recognize their order and ensure its continued viability

Around 150 years later, in 1244, the Holy Grail was in the Cathar castle of Montsegur in the Languedoc region of France. The Cathars removed it before the castle fell to the Pope's army

One theory that has been put forward is that the Knights Templars were Gnostic mystics who did not believe material things were important. Gnostics claim to possess a higher knowledge than others and believe real life exists only in the spiritual world, so anything done in the material world, even a grave sin, has no meaning.

For this reason, they were at odds with Christians. Whereas Christians believe that the source of truth is the Bible, Gnostics follow a different set of gospels. There are numerous contradictions between the two and Christians decry Gnostics' beliefs as false doctrines.

Gnosticism is based on a mystical approach to truth and questions most things that Christians believe in. Since these types of belief were likely to risk persecution by the church, the Knights Templars were forced to hide their beliefs in secret codes.

According to this theory, rather than the Holy Grail being a physical chalice, it is more likely that it stood for something else, which is claimed to be a spiritual heart or the heart of Jesus. That, in turn, represents a document written by Jesus of his teachings, which is what is believed likely to have been hidden somewhere.

Back as early as the Fifth Century, the spiritual heart was symbolized as being a drinking vessel. It's thought likely, therefore, that the Knights Templars were referring to the heart of Jesus when they mentioned the Grail.

The Naj Hammadi library, found in a cave in Egypt in 1947, contained documents that were written by Mary Magdalene and Thomas. This adds weight to the theory that the Grail may be a document of Jesus' writings. The fact that little is known of it is put down to it containing secret teachings intended only for His disciples.

Whatever it is and whether it even existed, the belief is that the Knights Templars were somehow involved. And the location of the Holy Grail, if it exists, is still a mystery.

Chapter 3: Conspiracy Theories And The

Location Of The Holy Grail Today

Many experts will tell you that the Holy Grail only exists in the imagination of writers, often historians who have a book they want to promote. Nevertheless, there are numerous people who claim to know the actual location of the Holy Grail, although many of those have little believable evidence to back up their claims.

All these claims should almost certainly be treated with a degree of skepticism based on the fact that various others have little credibility. There are, for example, several hundred nails in various locations that are believed to have been used in the crucifixion of Jesus. Similarly, there is enough wood in existence that is claimed to have been part of His cross to have made several crosses and with plenty to spare.

In terms of the Holy Grail itself, there are reported to be over two hundred claimed instances in Europe alone, with many more in other parts of the world. Whilst many of these claims can be dismissed out of hand, some do at least have a grain of credibility and others deserve serious consideration due to them at least being from the correct period.

The search for the Holy Grail has endured for more than seven hundred years and has not resulted in one definite and universally acclaimed outcome. Indeed, most of the claims have been demonstrably bogus although a small number are at least worth looking at. Many of these relate to artefacts that are stored in churches while others are in a diverse number of locations.

One of these is a chalice in Antioch Cathedral that, when first recovered in 1910, was claimed to be the Holy Grail. However, it was soon recognized to be too big to be a cup used at the Last Supper and has been identified as a Sixteenth Century standing lamp. It is now at the Metropolitan Museum of Art in New York.

Rosslyn Chapel, Scotland

This location was made famous by Dan Brown's novel, The Da Vinci Code, which was subsequently made into a film. In it, Brown claimed that the Holy Grail was located beneath the Collegiate Chapel of St. Matthew on Roslin Hill, in secret underground stone chambers.

The claim is backed up to some degree by the large number of unusual carvings in and around the building, including some pre-Christian images and carvings of maize, which was unknown in Europe at the time of the start of the chapel's construction in 1456. Building was instigated by nobleman and Knight William Sinclair, who was supposedly a Knights Templar descendent. One significant feature of the chapel is the unique Apprentice Pillar, which is said to stand over the Holy Grail

An alternative theory is that the Grail is kept in the sealed family crypt below the basement. Neither of these claims is ever likely to be proved, however, since the Sinclair family, which still owns the chapel, will not let the building be demolished to find what is within or beneath it.

The theory that the Knights Templar hid the Holy Grail at Rosslyn Chapel did not gain any credence until the 1960s. However, it was given a major boost by the publication of the Dan Brown novel and the location experienced a doubling of visitor numbers as a result. This is despite that fact that the novel, which is after all a work of fiction, went on to claim that the Holy Grail was relocated to the Inverted Pyramid besides the Louvre Museum in Paris.

Wales

One of the later claims to the location of the Holy Grail, which surfaced as recently 2006, is that Wales rather than Scotland is the likely site. Although no specific location is named, Welsh folklore specialist Doctor Juliette Wood of Cardiff University believes frequent references to Wales in Arthurian stories provide evidence of its likely presence there.

Although Doctor Wood is skeptical about the existence of the Holy Grail, she believes the legends that surround it are an important element of Welsh heritage. Owen Morgan, a bard and former journalist, theorizes that the Holy Grail represents the landscape of Wales rather than being a physical object.

Nanteos Cup, Wales

Still within Wales, it is believed that an artefact known as the Nanteos Cup is actually the Holy Grail. One version of the tale of the ancient relic is that it was brought to Britain in the 1300s by the Knights Templar and subsequently came into the possession of the Powell family who lived outside Aberystwyth on the Nanteos Estate.

Some believe the Nanteos Cup was made from the wood of Jesus' cross and has great healing powers as a result. Its first location in England was a church in Glastonbury, from where it was taken by monks to Wales on the dissolution of the monasteries by Henry VIII.

It was passed to an occupant of Nanteos House by the last surviving monk before his death and eventually came into the possession of the Powell family in the middle of the Nineteenth Century. They began to promote the healing properties of the relic and it became known as the Welsh Holy Grail from 1905.

The remains of the dark wooden cup, which measures 10 centimeters by 8.5 centimeters, has had pieces bitten from it by people who believed in its healing powers. It was originally kept behind glass by the Powell family and was reputedly exhibited at St. David's College, Lampeter, in 1870 when its healing powers become more widely known.

Descendents of the original occupants of the estate supposedly kept the cup in a bank vault for a time but then loaned it to a woman who was seriously ill. The relic was stolen from the Ross-on-Wye address but was subsequently recovered by police and returned to its owners.

Recovery of the relic occurred after a combined reward of £2,000 was put up for its safe return and an appeal was made on the TV programme Crimewatch. This resulted in an anonymous source coming forward and the cup being handed over, although no culprits were apprehended.

Prior to the cup being recovered, police raided a nearby public house after receiving intelligence but discovered nothing more than a wooden salad bowl. During the investigation, the police were keen to point out that they had not been hunting for the Holy Grail but were merely after a treasured possession that had been stolen.

Despite the claims that the Nanteos Cup is the Holy Grail, experts have cast serious doubts. They believe it is instead a mazer bowl, a domestic vessel that dates from the Fourteenth Century.

Glastonbury Tor, England

According to legend, the Knights Templar brought the Holy Grail to England after the First Crusade along with other relics they had captured. The Grail was then supposedly buried in Glastonbury Tor, a conical hill that is said to be the fabled Avalon from the Arthurian tales.

Tradition has it that King Arthur and Guinevere were buried there and their coffins were subsequently claimed to have been found by monks in 1191 at the top of the hill. The position of the bodies was marked with a cross that had a Latin inscription — 'Here lies buried the renowned King Arthur in the Isle of Avalon'. The finding of the graves was credited with sparking an interest in stories about King Arthur and the quest for the Holy Grail.

The fact the Holy Grail may be buried alongside Arthur and Guinevere is attractive to romanticists but there is no evidence to support any of this. The hill has been known as 'the Isle of Avalon' since 1100 AD, however, and it was used as a fort around 600 AD.

Lincoln Cathedral, England

Some scenes from The Da Vinci Code were filmed in Lincoln Cathedral so it is perhaps ironic that it is now claimed to be the Holy Grail's final resting place. This claim is made by EC Coleman, a retired naval officer but also a writer of historical books and leader of several expeditions.

Although representatives of the Cathedral are somewhat skeptical about the claim, Coleman has published a book about his findings and believes the evidence is clear. He maintains that the Knights Templar, with their powers in decline by 1280, gave the Grail to Bishop Oliver Sutton of Lincoln Cathedral.

When the Bishop died in 1299, the relic was placed alongside him in his tomb. In 1889, when the Cathedral was being repaired, workmen found the hidden tomb and discovered a chalice next to the skeleton.

The chalice is 4.5 inches high, made of silver and has no adornments. It is now in the cathedral's treasury and is available for the public to view.

The Dome of the Rock, Jerusalem, Israel

This version of events states that, after the Holy Grail was used to catch the blood of Jesus on the cross, it was buried alongside

Him in His tomb. Although the site of the tomb is not known, it is believed to be on or near the hill where the Dome of the Rock is located.

The site is sacred to Christians who believe Jesus' cross was placed a fissure between two rocks there. It is also sacred to Jews who think Abraham almost slew Isaac there, and to Muslims who claim Mohammed leapt from there to Heaven on a horse.

Sewers, Jerusalem

According to this theory, the Holy Grail was hidden, along with the Ark of the Covenant, in 586 BC to protect them from Nebuchadnezzar. The sewer system was an impenetrable maze and likely to be the best place to hide such sacred objects.

As a result of this deception, the Knights Templars were alleged never to have found the Holy Grail or the Ark of Covenant, which may still be where they were hidden. The truth of this is not likely to be revealed, however, since digging is forbidden, except for professional archaeologists, to prevent buildings being undermined.

The Hawkstone Chalice, England

In this version of events, the Holy Grail was owned by the Perevel family of Shropshire from the Middle Ages. It was eventually passed down to Thomas Wright, a Nineteenth Century writer, who claimed it was the Holy Grail.

Wright hid the chalice in Hawkstone Park and wrote a poem, Sir Gavain and the Red Knight, which contained clues to its whereabouts. This eventually led to its discovery, many years later, by local resident Graham Phillips, who found it inside the statue of an eagle.

All the mystery that surrounds the chalice does give it some attraction and the relic has been dated as First Century AD, which is around the right time. Nevertheless, the small egg cup shaped vessel, which is made of green alabaster, has been identified by the British Museum as a Roman scent jar.

Shugborough Hall, England

This Staffordshire property isn't claimed to be the location of the Holy Grail, but of an inscription on a statue that provides a coded indication of its whereabouts. The Eighteenth Century statue bears the letters O U O S V A V V and numerous unsuccessful attempts have been made to decipher the meaning.

Historian AJ Morton rather spoilt the speculation by claiming that half of the letters matched the initials of people living at Shugborough Hall. Although that claim has been denied by many, it is just an example of a code being linked to the Holy Grail for no real reason.

Cattedrale di San Lorenzo, Genoa, Italy

The candidate here is a green glass bowl that came via a mosque in Caesarea, Israel, where it was known to be in 1101. The bowl had previously been obtained at great cost in the Crusades and was originally thought to have been emerald until it was revealed to be green glass when dropped while being brought back from Paris after the fall of Napoleon. It is on public view but has not been carbon dated so its likely authenticity is unclear.

Santa Maria de Montserrat, Catalonia, Spain

The monastery and abbey of Montserrat are set in remote and rugged mountain terrain and the Grail is said to be located either under the church grounds or elsewhere on the surrounding mountain. Consequently, the scale and difficulty of the area — the peak rises to 4,055 feet — mean the chances of ever finding the Grail are probably nil.

There are, nevertheless, reasons for associating the area with the Holy Grail. The mountain, for example, is known as Sant Jeroni (Saint Jerome), who is mentioned in many of the Grail tales.

Additionally, there is a German legend of Munsalvaesche (or Corbenic), which refers to the castle where Sir Galahad was born and which was the home of the Fisher King. However, Munsalvaesche translates as 'the mount of salvation' whereas Montserrat means 'jagged mountain', so maybe the connection is a little contrived.

Catedral de Santa Maria de Valencia, Spain

If the Holy Grail really does exist, this is considered by many to be one of the strongest candidates for its location. Indeed, the city guide on the ValenciaValencia.com website states that all other claims have been dismissed and evidence from historians indicates that this is the genuine article. Archaeologists believe it is a Middle Eastern stone vessel dating from the First Century and that it possibly originated from Antioch in modern day Turkey.

The item in question is a cup known as the Santo Caliz, about 9 centimetres in diameter, made of dark red agate stone. This was a popular material for making drinking vessels at the time of Christ, although gold and pearl decorations have been added to the stem over the centuries since it was made.

The Santo Caliz is believed to have been initially taken to Rome where it was used as a Papal Chalice. Anticipating persecution, it was taken to Huesca in Spain in the Third Century and was not heard of during the Muslim occupation but then reappeared in several monasteries and churches as well as royal palaces. It was presented to Valencia Cathedral in the Fifteenth Century and can be viewed there.

The chalice is thought to be of Egyptian or Palestinian origin and was made between the Fourth Century BC and the First Century AD, which fits in with the theory of what it is. A document of 1134 describes it as the vessel in which 'Christ our Lord consecrated his blood' and it is the official chalice of the Roman Catholic Church, having been used to celebrate Mass by two Popes, most recently by Pope Benedict XVI in 2006.

Basilica of San Isidoro, Leon, Spain

One of the latest claims to the location of the Holy Grail, in early 2014, is made by a medieval history lecturer and an art historian, both conveniently based in the city of Leon in northern Spain. Even more conveniently, they're both written a book on the subject, which they were keen to promote.

Their claim is partly based on the contents of two medieval Egyptian parchments, describing how the Holy Grail was taken from Jerusalem to Cairo. It was given as a reward to an emir in Muslim Spain and then, in the Eleventh Century, was presented to King Fernando.

The chalice had been at the basilica for almost 1,000 years, hidden in another antique vessel called the Chalice of Dona Urruca. Made of onyx with gold and precious stones, it has been dated as being made between 200 BC and 100 AD.

Although nothing is known about the first four hundred years of the chalice's existence and there is no concrete proof it is the real Holy Grail, the finders remain convinced. Any doubts haven't stopped visitors flocking to see the chalice, forcing curators to remove it from view until a larger exhibition space could be found.

Fort Knox, Kentucky, USA

One of the more bizarre claims is that the Holy Grail is stored in the US Bullion Depositary at Fort Knox. That's not based on any particular evidence but purely on the fact that it's probably the most secure place there is and so appropriate to store such a valuable item.

According to the tale, the main vault has a special room that is used to hold the Ark of the Covenant, the True Cross and satellite photographs that show the Arafat Anomaly is Noah's Ark, as well as the Holy Grail. This is given slight credibility by the fact the vault has previously held the US Constitution and Declaration of Independence, a copy of the Magna Carta, the Hungarian crown jewels, the crown of Saint Stephen and various historical documents.

Security comprises electrified fences, alarms, cameras, armed guards and 30,000 active troops nearby who have equipment that includes Apache helicopter gunships, Abram tanks and armored personnel carriers. Other measures are likely to include land mines, snipers and motion activated gun turrets.

At 22 tons of steel, the main vault door can supposedly withstand a two kiloton nuclear strike and access to the property is limited to US Mint Police stationed there. The vault is lined with granite and has a ten-combination lock, each combination known only by one person working there.

Many people believe it is just too much security for something as simple as gold, hence the speculation that the property houses a much more valuable commodity.

Oak Island, Nova Scotia, USA

A so-called 'Money Pit', discovered in 1795, is guarded by a water channel booby trap and was originally thought to contain pirate treasure. Six people have so far died trying to find what the treasure is, lying exactly 100 feet down and described as 'metal in pieces'.

Speculation has grown over the years to the extent it is now thought the Knights Templar hid the Holy Grail there in the 1300s. This belief has been increased by the nearby presence of a perfect cross, formed out of boulders and measuring 250 by 100 meters.

According to legend, a seventh person has to die in the pit before its secret is revealed.

Accokeek, Maryland, USA

The rumor here is that the Holy Grail was taken by treasure seekers from its hiding place on Glastonbury Tor. It was taken by a Jesuit priest to America, up the Potomac River to Accokeek.

This all occurred around 1606-07 and the priest supposedly had ties going back to the Knights Templar. However, the location of the Holy Grail is not specified and little else is known.

The Holy Grail in Modern Culture

Although many of the stories about the Holy Grail were written in the Middle Ages, covering the Arthurian legends and other romantic tales, there are several instances from the Twentieth Century forward. Perhaps the best known of these in recent times are two films — The Da Vinci Code and Indiana Jones and the Last Crusade.

The former, based on Dan Brown's bestselling novel, follows the theory that Jesus did not die but had children with Mary Magdalene. In the story, their descendants founded the Merovingian dynasty and live on to this day and the revelation undermines the foundation on which the Roman Catholic Church is based. The novel and film traced the Holy Grail to Rosslyn Chapel in Scotland, from where it was supposedly moved by its guardians to a secret chamber in the floor underneath the Inverted Pyramid besides the Louvre Museum in Paris.

The theory of Jesus' blood line had earlier been featured in the 'Priory of Sion' hoax and was then described in the 1982 publication Holy Blood, Holy Grail, which was rather treated as a work of fiction.

In Indiana Jones and the Last Crusade, the hero undertakes a modern day search for the Grail. Here, the story reflected in part actual events, the Nazis under Adolf Hitler having supposedly being obsessed with finding the fabled city of Atlantis as well as the Holy Grail.

This was part of an attempt to rediscover the lost Aryan race in order to establish a new religion and develop a truly pure and superior race. The attempt was the responsibility of an SS unit known as Ahnenerbe (Ancestral

Heritage) that scoured the world looking for the city of Atlantis and the Grail.

Archaeologist Herman Wirth started the process by claiming to know the location of Atlantis. He discovered symbols that he believed indicated the survivors of Atlantis, a superior race, had fled to different parts of the world, particularly Tibet.

Files found after the end of the war documented the work of the Ahnenerbe and their conclusion that Tibetans were descended from Aryans. That prompted a quest to achieve racial purity, which perhaps led to the launch of the Holocaust.

According to a Channel 5 television programme, Nazi Quest for the Holy Grail, Otto Rahn, a historian who led a search for the Grail, concluded that its last keepers were the Cathars, who were wiped out in the Thirteenth Century.

He determined that the Holy Grail was located at Montsegur, a ruined castle in the French Pyrenees. Heinrich Himmler, the leader of the SS who believed that possession of the Holy Grail would help the Nazis win the war, apparently visited another possible site, Montserrat Abbey in north east Spain. He was so confident that the Holy Grail would eventually be found that an empty plinth was reserved for it in a castle in Westphalia.

Rahn was an eccentric who wore a black fedora hat and was almost certainly the inspiration for the character Indiana Jones in Steven Spielberg's series of films. He was, like Jones, obsessed with finding the Holy Grail.

He was apparently an honorable man who only joined the SS so he would be able to continue his work. However, he eventually became so disillusioned with the true nature of the organization that he tried to resign from it. His punishment for this was to be posted as a guard at a concentration camp, where he eventually swallowed a handful of sleeping pills, walked out into the snow and froze to death

Other recent films on the subject include the comic adaptation, Monty Python and the Holy Grail, which was itself adapted as a stage production with the title Spamalot. The Fisher King was a parody of the story that set the quest for the Grail in modern times, while earlier versions include Lancelot du Lac in 1974 and The Light of Faith (1922), in which Lon Chaney tried to steal the Holy Grail.

The earliest known mention of the Holy Grail in films was in the silent Parsifal while The Silver Chalice was a 1954 film based on a novel of the same name. TV series Babylon 5 and Stargate SG-1 have also featured the Grail, the latter in an episode called 'The Quest'.

The continual retelling of the tale of the Holy Grail, albeit with ever more fictional additions and embellishments, keeps the subject within the public conscience. It ensures the ongoing fascination with this mysterious relic is unlikely to ever fade.

That fascination is driven partly by the supposed magical powers of the Holy Grail but mainly by the fact that is has never truly been found. It is the ultimate unobtainable object and, as such, will continue to tantalize future generations. Indeed, were it ever to be found and credible evidence of its authenticity were available, that would rather spoil the myth that has developed over the centuries.

The story of the Holy Grail is one that has been told over many centuries by a whole variety of people and consequently there are multiple versions of the tale. Its origins and initial use are shrouded in mystery, as is its very form, while various people are credited with bringing the Grail to Britain. The identity of the Fisher King varies with each book that you read, as does the hero credited with completing the Grail quest, and the current location of the Holy Grail, if there is one, is the biggest mystery of all.

Chapter 4: The Grail Christianized

And in the blast there smote along the hall

A beam of light seven times more clear than day:

And down the long beam stole the Holy Grail

All over covered with a luminous cloud.

And none might see who bare it, and it past.

In his story of the Grail, Chretien de Troyes does not tell us what the Grail is. But he does indicate that it is holy when he says that it contains a consecrated wafer, which is enough to support the life of the Fisher King's father. However, because he died before completing the story, the mystery has never been resolved and the meaning of the Grail has never been explained.

After him several authors attempted to write a continuation of the legend. With each retelling, it became more strongly linked with Christ until, in 1200, Robert de Boron wrote hisJoseph of Arimathea,based on the figure from the Bible.

JOSEPH OF ARIMATHEA

Joseph was born at Arimathea, a Judean city, and was a wealthy and influential man in first-century Palestine. He is thought to have been a senator, perhaps a member of the Sanhedrin, and the supreme council of the Jews. He was a secret disciple of Jesus because he was afraid of his position being compromised. However, after Jesus's crucifixion he asked Pontius Pilate to let him have the body of Christ. Permission being granted, he took the body to a tomb, hewed out of rock, that he had prepared for himself. His friend Nicodemus went with him and provided a quantity of spices for preparing the body, which they wrapped in linen and herbs. They then rolled a large stone over the entrance.

THE CUP OF CHRIST

Robert de Boron takes the story of Joseph of Arimathea and links it with the story of the Grail to form a strongly Christianized version. At the same time he defines the Grail, making it both a physical and a spiritual object. He says that at the same time as Joseph of

Arimathea acquired the body of Jesus, he also acquired the Cup of the Last Supper. This he uses to catch blood flowing from the body of Jesus. Afterwards he hides the cup in his house. Later, he is thrown into prison for his faith, but while he is languishing there, Christ appears to him and gives him the same cup, teaching him some holy words 'which are rightly called the secret of the Grail'. Joseph is miraculously sustained by food provided by the chalice, now identified as the Holy Grail, until he is finally released from prison.

The story then becomes very involved. Joseph gathers up his family, including his sister and her husband Brons, and takes them travelling. At one stage they almost die of hunger, but magically a fish caught by Brons is converted by the Grail into enough food for the entire company. After this, Brons becomes known as the Rich Fisher and is instructed by an angel to go west and await the arrival of his grandson, who will eventually receive the chalice as well as the secret words, so that he can understand its meaning.

This tale, although muddled and confusing, contains important new elements of the story. Firstly it links the Holy Grail with Christ through Joseph of Arimathea; secondly it attempts to explain the title of the Fisher King (at the same time suggesting an identification with Bran); and thirdly it seems to be concerned with some secret or mystery teachings concerning Christ.

THE QUESTE DEL SAINT GRAAL

De Boron's Joseph of Arimathea paved the way for the vast Christian text known as the Prose Lancelot or the Vulgate Cycle. This was the text on which Malory later based his famous version of the legends of King Arthur. The Vulgate Cycle is an anonymous compilation of Arthurian stories written in French in the early 1200s. Although ascribed to someone called Waiter Map, it is considered too extensive to be the work of one man and is now thought to have been written by a group of Cistercian monks. Certainly it reflects the teachings of their founder St Bernard of Clairvaux, who had a strong belief in the doctrine of grace and the mystical union of the soul with God.

The Cycle relates the entire story of King Arthur and his Knights leading up to the quest of the Grail. It also introduces, by a stroke of genius, the character of Galahad into the Arthurian legends. But in order to do so, it had to break the chivalric rules concerning adultery and chastity. The story is a curious one and concerns Lancelot's meeting with the Grail Maiden.

LANCELOT AND THE MAIDEN OF THE GRAIL

Lancelot comes upon the Castle of King Pelles (in some versions merged with King Pellam - see below), Here he meets the Grail Maiden, Elaine. With the connivance of her father, a powerful enchantress called Dame Brisen magically causes Elaine to take on the likeness of Queen Guinevere. In this way Lancelot is tricked into sleeping with her. The next morning, according to Malory, the 'fair lady Elaine skipped out of her bed all-naked, and kneeled down afore Sir Lancelot'. She begs him not to kill her for her deception because 'the noblest knight of all the world' is in her womb.

Lancelot forgives her and kisses her 'for she was as fair a lady, and they're to lusty and young'. Thus, out of the forbidden adulterous love between Lancelot and Guinevere, Galahad, the purest knight of all, is conceived.

GALAHAD COMES TO ARTHUR'S COURT

Having established the birth of Galahad, the true Grail hero, theVulgate Cyclegoes on to tell of his first appearance at Arthur's Court. The account begins with an old man (later identified as Merlin) bringing Galahad to the Round Table and leading him to theSiege Perilous,the Dangerous Seat that has been designated for the perfect knight. After taking this seat, Galahad further demonstrates his superiority by being the only knight able to draw a magic sword from a floating block of red marble. This initiatory ritual echoes that of Arthur pulling the sword from the stone. It indicates that the story is moving into a new dimension in which the perfect knight is required to possess spiritual qualities that outstrip the former courtly ones.

When all the knights have resumed their seats at the Round Table, a ferocious clap of thunder is heard, after which a shaft of dazzlingly bright sunlight enters and illuminates the entire hall. Everyone present is struck dumb and remains in this state for a long time until the Holy Grail appears, covered with a cloth of white samite but not carried by any human hand. Immediately the palace is filled with a fragrance 'as though all the spices of the earth had been spilled abroad'. But this vision is tantalizingly incomplete because the Grail remains covered. After the Grail has disappeared and the power of speech has returned to the knights, Gawain pledges himself to go on the quest of the Grail, and the flower of Arthur's knights follow suit.

The ladies of the court wish to accompany them but an old hermit enters the hall and tells them that no man can take a woman with him on the quest for it is 'no search for earthly things but a seeking out of the mysteries and hidden sweets of Our Lord'." Then Arthur, realizing this will mean the breaking up of the Fellowship of the Round Table, mourns the loss of his fair company. There follow the accounts of individual quests of the Grail in which the ultimate hero is now Galahad rather than Perceval. (For these see Chapter 4.)

THE LANCE OF LONGINUS

With the elaboration of the Arthurian Romances, not only was the Grail turned into the Cup of Christ, the blood-dripping spear was also Christianized. It was turned into the lance of Longinus, the Roman centurion who pierced Christ's side while he was on the Cross. Because the Cup of the Last Supper was also used by Joseph of Arimathea to catch the blood and water that issued from Christ's side, the connection between the two symbols - which the Celts had recognized - was cleverly preserved. Added to that, in order to make it sit happily in the Arthurian tradition, the lance was also linked with the one used by Sir Balin to deal theDolorous Stroke.

THE DOLOROUS STROKE

This extraordinary story tells how Balin sets out on a quest and encounters Garlon, King Pellam's brother, who is said to be both black-faced and invisible. Because of his invisibility he can pick off other knights undetected. In this way he slays Balin's companion. Angrily, Balin rides on to the Castle of Carbonek (the Grail Castle), where he avenges his friend by killing Garlon with a well-aimed swipe of his sword. King Pellam immediately turns on Balin to avenge his brother. Balin breaks his sword in trying to defend himself and runs through the castle from chamber to chamber looking for a weapon, with King Pellam hard on his heels.

At last Balin comes into a rich chamber containing a bed and a gold table on silver legs. On this table is a 'marvelous spear strangely wrought'. Without pausing for thought, he snatches up the spear and strikes King Pellam with it, whereupon the King swoons and the castle roof and walls fall down. Balin and the Pellam lie under the rubble for three days until Merlin comes and rescues them. But Pellam continues to languish from his wound, waiting for Galahad's achievement of the Grail quest to restore his health.

JOSEPH OF ARIMATHEA COMES TO GLASTONBURY

In some of the later Grail accounts, the Grail King is identified with Joseph of Arimathea. Because of the Grail stories, Joseph became very important and there is an apocryphal tradition concerning him, which says he was the uncle of the Virgin Mary and therefore a relative of Jesus. This same legend goes on to tell how after the Crucifixion Joseph travelled to Gaul on a preaching mission, accompanied by a band of Christians who included the Apostle Philip, Lazarus and Mary Magdalene. They stopped off at the south of France, where Mary Magdalene disembarked with some of the company, while the others kept travelling north until they reached England. Their boat ran aground at the Glastonbury marshes so they got out and climbed a hill in order to see the lie of the land.

Legend says that Joseph then thrust his staff (grown from Christ's Crown of Thorns) into the ground, declaring that they were all weary, whereupon it is said to have miraculously taken root and budded. After this, Joseph met with the ruler of Britain, Ariviragus, and was granted twelve hides of land at Glastonbury in order to establish the first monastery in Britain. His early wattle church was dedicated to the Virgin Mary but was unfortunately burned down in 1184. A few years later, however, with the supposed finding of Arthur's tomb, Glastonbury became such a great place of pilgrimage and attracted such revenue that the monks could afford to build the great abbey - the ruins of which still exist there.

By this time, owing to his founding of the first Christian Church, Joseph of Arimathea had become a saint and acquired cult status. Meanwhile a strong belief had arisen around him which said that he had brought the Chalice, or Cup of Christ, with him and that it was buried somewhere at Glastonbury.

APPLICATION - A PILGRIMAGE TO GLASTONBURY

It is helpful for the Grail questor to visit some of the holy sites connected with the Grail legend. This is because he or she will encounter the energies of others on the quest. It will also involve the questor at a physical as well as a spiritual level in the search for the Grail. Glastonbury is a place highly charged with spiritual energy. Whether you believe the Grail can be found there or not, going to Glastonbury will be an important and instructive pilgrimage. The following visualization is a preparation for your visit, but can also be used by those who are unable to get there physically.

VISUALIZATION

You begin your pilgrimage at the ancient Abbey, the place where Joseph of Arimathea built his church. Entering the ruins, you walk among half-rubbled walls, past arches and tall windows, through the long 'Galilee' to reach the Lady Chapel at the far end. Look up at the three perpendicular windows above you. This is where the first wattle church stood, dedicated to the Virgin Mary. There is peace here and great stillness. Ponder her wisdom.

Below the chapel is the crypt, dedicated to Joseph of Arimathea. This was once a dark and secret place with a mysterious well in a far dark corner. Imagine it as it once was and ponder the secret words that Joseph received from Jesus.

When you areready make your way down the nave and through the tall broken archway into the choir. Go towards the high altar and stop at the grave of Arthur and Guinevere. Here were unearthed the bones of a giant of a man and the bones of a woman with a plaited lock of blonde hair. Yet tradition says Arthur has no grave and will come again. Even if this was not the grave of Arthur, stop and remember him. His court was worthy of the Grail, his knights worthy of its quest. He is still a power in the land.

Outside the Abbey you will find the Glastonbury Thorn, which took root from the staff of Joseph of Arimathea. This is grown from a slip of the first thorn tree, which was cut down by a zealous Puritan. It still flowers out of season.

There are many ways from the Abbey to the Tor, which is where you are next headed. The route along Dod Lane is green and pretty and will take you straight to that extraordinary landmark. As you climb you see above you the ruins of St Michael's chapel, and the landscape spreading out below. Others are climbing with you, all believing in the spiritual presence there. You reach the top and sit and rest near the ruins looking out over the flat lands around you. You might like to think about the power and beauty of the land, how it was once a lake, perhaps the mystical lake over which the dark barge sailed taking the dying Arthur to be healed. Three mysterious queens took him and he disappeared with them into the haze above the water.

When you are ready, descend the Tor and make your way to Chalice Well at the. foot of Chalice Hill. You reach it through the beautiful and peaceful Chalice Gardens. The well is fed by a spring from which 25,000 gallons of pure water flow daily. The water is believed to have healing powers. Nearby is the White Spring. This also has healing powers. Drink from it. You are drinking theElixir Vitae,the Waters of Life. Now go back and look deep into the waters of the Chalice Well. Is this where the Grail is hidden?

Joseph of Arimathea among the Rocks of Albion,William Blake

Chapter 5: Grail Quests

Thequest of the Grail was no ordinary one. Knights who had been used to their prowess and chivalry being tested were unprepared for the nature of such a quest. It went beyond bravery and skills in arms, beyond magic and beyond the psychological, and entered the realm of the spiritual. Of some 150 knights who set out on the quest, only five knights and one woman are reported to have come anywhere near to achieving it. There are also differing accounts of their quests, which report varying degrees of success. Their individual experiences are detailed below. Some of the accounts are complex, so you may like to pick one or two for reading now and come back later to the others. Or you may like to read them all quickly and then return to the ones that you wish to work with. This chapter is intended to repay deeper study over a period of time.

GAWAIN

Gawain is one of the original knights from the Celtic stories of Arthur. His Welsh name is Gwaichmai, which means Hawk of May. He was Arthur's nephew and champion and, in fact, would have been next in line to Arthur's throne according to the Celtic system of succession. In the earliest stories of the Grail quest his adventures intertwine with those of Perceval, and some scholars think he may have been the original Grail hero. But by the time Malory wrote his version of the Grail story, Gawain had been superseded as chief knight of the realm, first by Lancelot and then by Galahad.

GAWAIN'S QUEST

At the beginning of Malory's account, Gawain is weary, having set out a long time before and as yet found no meaningful adventure. He meets up with Sir Ector and they ride together until they come to a derelict chapel. They enter to pray and then fall asleep. Gawain has a dream in which he sees 150 bulls. All of them are black except for three, which are white, and one of these bears a black spot. Sir Ector also has a strange dream. When they both awake a mysterious hand and forearm, covered in red samite and holding a brightly burning candle, appears and passes in front of them entering the chapel and then vanishing. A voice tells them that they are both lacking in faith and will not achieve theSangratl.

They decide to go to Nacien the hermit for an explanation. On their way Gawain jousts with a knight and kills him. He discovers, too late, that he was Sir Uwain who was also on the quest of the Grail. Nacien the hermit explains Gawain's dream, which means that only three knights are worthy of the quest. Two, Perceval and Galahad are pure, while the third, Bors, is chaste, having only slept with a woman once. The candle symbolizes the Holy Ghost.

After this, Gawain meets Sir Galahad, who smites him so hard that his sword goes through his helmet and into his head. Then Galahad disappears. Gawain, realizing that this stroke has been dealt him because he tried to pull the sword from the red marble slab, decides to stop seeking the Grail.

In this account Galahad appears like an avenging angel. He has not only superseded Gawain in pulling out the magic sword, but will also succeed in the quest where Gawain fails. However, three earlier accounts give Gawain better success. One is the first continuation of Chretien de Troyes's original story, written by Gautier de Danans.

In this version Gawain stops to pray in a chapel and sees a great black hand appear and put out the altar light. He later arrives at the Grail Castle and goes into a room, which contains the body of a knight holding a Cross and a Broken Sword. He dines that night with the Fisher King and sees the Grail procession. He is given the Broken Sword and asked to restore it (rather like Perceval in other accounts), but his failure to do so renders him unfit for the quest. He manages, however, to ask the meaning of the lance and is told it is the one, which pierced Christ's side on the Cross. He falls asleep and awakes on the seashore surrounded by flowering countryside that has magically recovered because he learned the answer to one question. More would have been achieved if he could have asked about the Grail itself.

The motif of the sword is echoed in another account in the French text called thePerlesvaus.Here Gawain is only allowed to enter the Grail Castle once he has obtained the sword that beheaded St John the Baptist, which bleeds every day at noon. He finds the sword and witnesses the Grail procession, in which the shape of a child appears in the center of the Grail. Three drops of blood drip onto the table in front of him and he becomes captivated by the sight and unable to speak. After this he sees the Grail high in the air and above it Christ nailed to the Cross with a spear in his side. He is so moved by this sight that, like Perceval, he fails to ask the question that would heal the land. He is then transported to the Castle with a magic chessboard (see Chapter 7).

In this story the motifs of the broken sword, the magic game of chess and the episode of the three drops of blood, are so similar to the adventures of Perceval, that it seems the two heroes were at one time interchangeable. As if to confirm this, there is one version in which Gawain does succeed in the quest. This is in Diu Crone (The Crown) by Heinrich von dem Tulin. He tells how Gawain and Lancelot witness the Grail procession together, but Lancelot falls asleep so it is left to Gawain to ask the correct questions about the Grail. He does so and at once all those present, both the living and the dead, are released from their enchantments.

LANCELOT'S QUEST

Lancelot initially sets out on the quest with Perceval. They meet Galahad, who is disguised, and each jousts with him. Galahad gets the better of them and then rides away so quickly that they are unable to catch up with him. After this Lancelot goes on alone until he comes to a crossroads at the edge of the Waste Land. Beside it is a derelict chapel, but inside the chapel Lancelot can see a rich altar with a six-branched silver candlestick on it, which gives out a bright light. Lancelot finds he is unable to enter the chapel and instead falls asleep on his shield outside.

Lancelot then sees in a visionary dream a sick knight lying in a litter mourning for the presence of the holy vessel that will heal him. Then the Holy Grail appears and the knight sits up and kisses it and is immediately healed. The Grail then passes into the chapel. Lancelot is powerless to move. When he finally awakes he finds his helmet and sword have gone and he hears a voice that tells him he is harder than stone, more bitter than wood and more naked than the leaf of the fig tree.

He travels to a hermitage and is told by the hermit that his sin with Guinevere has prevented his achieving the Grail. He repents and travels on until he comes to the sea. He is told in a dream to enter a ship. The ship magically appears and he boards it to find a dead woman lying on a bed with a letter in her hand. (This is Dindrane, Perceval's sister - see page 36.) Galahad joins him on the ship and they spend half a year in each other's company meeting with adventures on various islands until Galahad is summoned by a White Knight to leave the ship.

Eventually Lancelot finds the Grail Castle and has to brave a pair of fierce lions by means of faith rather than prowess. Inside he finds the Grail Chamber but is unable to enter. He sees through the doorway the Holy Vessel covered with red samite, as well as a host of angels and a priest saying mass. The priest lifts up the body of a man as if it were the Host. Without thinking, Lancelot rushes forward to help him with the body, but feels as if he has met a wall of fire, and swoons. He is carried out of the chamber. Next day he is found as if dead and carried to a bed where he lies unable to open his eyes for twenty-four days. After recovering he is told that he is in the Castle of Carbonek. The Fisher King treats him with great respect. However, he is told that he has achieved as much of theSangrailas is possible for him, and so he returns to Arthur's court.

BORS'S QUEST

Sir Bors sets off on the quest and meets Nacien the hermit riding on an ass. He receives instruction from the hermit, who clothes him in a red gown. Bors determines to eat nothing but bread and water until he has achieved the quest. He rides on and comes to a parting of two ways. There he sees a naked man on horseback being beaten with thorns by two knights. The man looks up and Bors realizes with horror that it is his brother Sir Lionel. At the same time he hears the cries of a beautiful maiden who is being carried off by a knight on horseback in the other direction. Bors is torn between his duty to his brother and his oath to defend all women who call upon him. He decides to rescue the maiden and chases after her abductor, overcoming him and killing him. He then escorts her back to her castle.

Later he comes to a castle with a high tower. There he is made welcome by the Lady and her twelve women companions and offered rich food. However, he will eat only bread and water because of his vow. Then the Lady asks him to sleep with her. When he refuses, she says that if he will not love her, she and her maidens will all ascend the tower and jump off. Sir Bors is again in a dilemma but sticks to his decision, whereupon they all jump. When they immediately disappear with much shrieking, Bors realizes that he was being tempted by an illusion.

After this he rides on and comes upon his brother, who has managed to escape from his oppressors. However, Lionel is so angry with Bors for not rescuing him that he threatens to kill him. Bors will not fight his brother and a hermit intervenes and is killed in his place. Lionel again attempts to kill Bors, but Bors draws his sword. Then a voice warns him not to kill his brother and a fiery cloud appears and burns both their shields. They both fall down in a swoon. When they recover, Lionel begs Bors to forgive him, which he does gladly, before riding away.

Bors then comes to the sea and boards a ship, on which he finds Perceval. Galahad joins them and Bors becomes one of the company of successful knights who achieve the Grail and also travel to the Holy City of Sarras. Bors eventually returns to Arthur's court to tell of the quest.

DINDRANE'S QUEST

Dindrane is Perceval's sister who becomes part of the Grail company on the magic ship. Although she does not achieve the Grail, she fails for the noblest of reasons.

Dindrane appears inPerlesvausas a mysterious but saintly figure, then again in Malory. She guides Sir Galahad to the magic ship and boards it with him. They find Perceval and Bors already on it. She then acts as guide to all three of them and instructs them to board another ship. Then she reveals to Perceval that she is his sister. She shows them the strange objects on the ship, a rich bed, a crown and a sword, and says that only Galahad is worthy to draw the sword. She then gives them explanations for the strange objects. The sword is the sword of David, and the bed is the Tree of Life, linked with Adam and Eve and also with King Solomon. She then makes new girdles, or hangings, for the sword using her own hair.

The four of them come to a castle and are constrained to go in because the custom of the castle forbids any virgin to pass without giving a dish of her blood. This is because the lady of the castle has been languishing from leprosy for many years and has been told that this is how she will be healed. Dindrane willingly gives her blood and dies as a result, although the lady of the castle is healed. In this strange feminine mirroring of the Fisher King's malady, Dindrane's blood caught in the silver dish becomes the equivalent of the Grail and her sacrificial death is like that of Galahad when he achieves the Grail.

Dindrane makes a final request. Before she dies she asks that her body be put in a barge covered in black silk and left to the mercy of the sea. She prophesies that she will arrive at the City of Sarras (see below) before the other three and asks them to bury her there. Perceval writes an account of their strange adventures and puts it in her right hand. This is how she is found by Lancelot when he himself boards a boat before being joined by Galahad. This is a curious inversion of the tale of the Fair Maid of Astolat (the Lady of Shalott), who died for love of Lancelot and was put in a barge covered in black samite that floated down to Camelot.

Although Dindrane does not achieve the Grail, there is a compelling episode inPerlesvausin which she has a foretaste of it. This is when, all alone, she braves the horrible Perilous Cemetery, which is haunted by the ghosts of unrepentant Black Knights. She passes through it and eventually reaches the chapel in the middle, finding it filled with light. There she has a vision of the Virgin Mary and sees

a holy clothe on the chapel altar. It rises up in the air but she begs to be allowed to have some of the cloth, which she knows is the shroud that was used to wrap the body of Christ. The cloth descends to the altar and she is given a portion of it. This strange story in which Dindrane has to go alone and cannot be accompanied by her brother, suggests it is connected with the Feminine Mysteries, or ancient secret religious practices.

PERCEVAL'S QUEST

In the early stories Perceval is presented as a type of Perfect Fool. His naivety and innocence are part of what fits him for the role of hero. He acquires prowess and courtliness as he journeys towards his destiny. Although his story breaks off or is unconvincingly wrapped up in the two earliest versions, in some continuations he achieves the Grail quest a second time, asks the Question and brings about the healing of the Fisher King. There are also accounts of his replacing the Fisher King as the keeper of the Grail and taking Blancheflor as his wife.

In thePerlesvaus,Perceval has his own adventures alone on board a magical ship which takes him to several mysterious islands, one of which contains a community of thirty-three priestly men who seem like an inner circle of initiates (see Chapter 6). In this version he becomes the Grail King and returns to rule an Elysian Island of Plenty.

In the later versions found in theVulgate Cycleand in Malory, Perceval is superseded by Galahad but becomes linked with him and Sir Bors when all three travel on the magical

Ship of Solomon in the final stages of the Grail quest. Although he outlives Galahad by just over a year, dying in a hermitage in Sarras, in this account he is really only a facet of Galahad.

GALAHAD'S QUEST

Although Galahad becomes the final Grail knight, he is hardly a human figure at all. He appears like an initiating angel to joust with Lancelot, Bors and Perceval when they are embarked on the Grail quest. After each occasion he miraculously disappears. He also at this time rides incognito carrying a white shield bearing a red cross that has been made by the blood of Joseph of Arimathea, issuing from his nose. Galahad is said to be a direct descendant of Joseph of Arimathea, as is his father, Lancelot.

There are two accounts of Galahad sailing on magic ships. In one he accompanies his father, and in this he can be seen as relating to or identifying with him. In fact it could be argued that Lancelot achieves the Grail through his son. Conversely, Galahad's spiritual achievement can also be seen as emanating from his father's physical prowess and courtliness. Certainly the flawed man and the spiritual one are linked.

When he boards the second ship Galahad becomes the leader of the trio of men who achieve the Grail together. Dindrane, who sails with them, is a type of the feminine spirit of wisdom who guides them. After splitting up and reuniting, the three knights eventually arrive at the Castle of Carbonek together and are presented with the Broken Sword. Galahad is the only one who can mend it but he then presents it to Bors.

Just before they see the Grail procession the Maimed King is carried in on 'a bed of tree', with a gold crown on his head. The Grail procession is led by a man who is said to be Joseph, the first Christian bishop who was comforted in the spiritual palace in the city of Sarras. Angels follow him bearing candles, a towel and a spear that bleeds into a box. According to Malory, the bishop lifts up a wafer resembling bread, whereupon the figure of a child with a face as bright as fire 'smote himself into the bread'.

The bread is returned to the holy vessel and changes into the bleeding body of Christ, who mystically gives himself as the Host to the three knights. They all partake of the Grail but it is Galahad who anoints the Maimed King with blood that has dripped from the lance, after which he is healed. The three knights are told by Christ to take the holy vessel to Sarras in order to experience its powers more fully.

This they do, but when they arrive they are immediately imprisoned by the King and, like Joseph of Arimathea, are kept alive only by the sustenance of the Grail. After a year, however, the King falls ill and asks their forgiveness. The King then dies and the people of Sarras are instructed by a disembodied voice to choose Galahad as his successor. After a year Galahad receives a mystical mass from Joseph of Arimathea and dies, whereupon he is carried up to

Heaven by angels along with the Grail and the Holy Lance. In this enactment of the Resurrection, Galahad is clearly shown to be a type of Christ, the Grail having been demonstrated as the Chalice of the Mass, containing the body as well as the blood of Christ.

The Grail Heroes

APPLICATION

As is evident from the accounts given above, the quests are all different, each being related to the deeds and character of the particular questor. It is important to remember that the quest is an individual one. This is why the road is often lonely. The knights were pitted against themselves in their efforts to reach the highest goal possible. Their only guides were the solitary hermits they encountered in the forests. There was no Church or ecclesiastical hierarchy to guide them because the path was not a general one.

You may like to choose one of the quests for meditation. They are complicated but will repay study. If you have difficulty choosing, these are the main characteristics of the different questors:

Gawain

The most ancient and Celtic of the questors, Gawain was the first to jump up and offer to go on the quest. He is spontaneous but sometimes lacks stamina. He is one of the most gentle and courteous of Arthur's knights. He is especially sensitive to the needs of women and is also merciful to vanquished enemies. He is one of the finest champions of

Arthur's court. Although in some tales he has the wit to give up the quest when he realizes it is not for him, hi others he wins through like Perceval.

Lancelot

This hero has reached the highest point possible in terms of prowess and skill in arms. His courtliness is also legendary. The trouble is that this extends to a love for Guinevere, which goes beyond the bounds of chivalry into adultery. He has therefore betrayed his king and curbed his own spiritual potential. He is the flawed hero.

Nevertheless he has two options. He can repent and give up his adulterous love, in which case he is not too late to achieve the full experience of the Grail, or he can continue his quest and accept a limited physical experience. In the end he opts for the limited experience. Nevertheless just by attempting the quest he encounters his unknown son and also achieves some experience of the Grail. However, this is almost too much for him and he takes a long time to recover from it. His quest can be seen therefore as both encouraging and cautionary.

Perceval

Considered the original Grail hero, Perceval is also naive and plays the part of the Fool, especially at the outset of his career. Nevertheless his initial innocence gives him special insight into the spiritual side of life. He is enthusiastic, like Gawain, but also has Otherworldly nobility, especially towards the end of his quest. In some accounts he not only achieves the Grail, but also becomes the Grail King, ruling over the restored land, together with his wife and two sons. He is able to combine spirituality, love and family life.

Bors

Bors is in some ways the least flamboyant and most down-to- earth of the questors. However, when he is preparing for his quest he does receive some strong visionary dreams. He is very determined. He finds decisions difficult but, when he has made up his mind, he sticks to it. He manages to resist the Lady's advances in the castle and he does his best in the impossible situation where he has to choose between helping his brother or the abducted maiden. He demonstrates great nobility when his brother nearly kills him and, as a result, is rescued by supernatural forces.

He is privileged to be part of the final trio accompanying Galahad on the last stages of the journey. Galahad considers him worthy of the mended sword. But, unlike Galahad, Bors is not so spiritual that he wishes to expire after achieving the Grail. He returns to Arthur's court to tell the story and resume a normal life.

Dindrane

Dindrane's experience is the least clear-cut/In some ways she does not really go on her own journey. She 'accompanies the three heroes on the final stages of their quest but gives up her life on the way. It seems as if she has already experienced the Grail and is closely involved with it in ways that the others have yet to discover. She has the gift of foreknowledge, which suggests that she is an Otherworldly figure.Inmeditation, she can be sought as a guide alongside any of the other questors. She also represents an inner experience of the Grail and of the feminine Mysteries, which lie deeper than words. She is a very powerful helper on the quest.

Galahad

Galahad is also an Otherworldly figure. He is too perfect to be human. Born solely for the Grail quest, he has inherited the prowess of his father but goes beyond him in spiritual attainment. He demonstrates a balance of masculine and feminine energies. In his warrior aspect he is a challenger, but he is also a healer, having healed the Fisher King.

In your strivings on your quest, take heart and encouragement from the great figures that have gone before you. Meet them in your meditations and learn from their experiences.

Chapter 6: The Gnostic Grail

Passionate, with longing inmyeyes,

Searching wide, and seeking nights and days,

Lo! I beheld the Truthful One, the Wise,

Here in mine own house to fillmygaze.

In Chapter 4we saw how, according to legend, Joseph of Arimathea travelled to England with the Holy Grail. He was accompanied by a band of Christian believers, among whom was Mary Magdalene. The company split into two groups, some staying behind in France, while Joseph and the others carried on to England. This has given rise to speculation that the Grail may have been buried at Glastonbury, possibly in or near the Chalice Well.

An alternative theory claims that the Grail stayed behind in France with Mary Magdalene. This provocative theory involves the cult of the Magdalene, as well as that of the Black Madonna, and not least the heretical faith of theCathars,who lived in the Languedoc area in the south of France.

MARY MAGDALENE

Mary Magdalene is known from the gospel stories as the woman from whom Jesus cast out seven devils and who thereafter became his close companion and follower. She is also often identified with the woman who anointed his feet with costly nard, or perfume, and wiped them with her hair. She was also present at the Crucifixion and she was the first person to see the risen Christ. Despite this honor, a strong tradition has grown up around her suggesting that she was a prostitute who was reformed by her contact with Christ, but this is not substantiated by the Bible.

Ancient texts have recently come to light, however, which seem to show that this portrayal of Mary Magdalene as a fallen woman is inaccurate. There is now a belief that the casting out of the seven devils may refer to an initiation ceremony that she had undergone as part of an Egyptian Mystery Religion, the Cult of Isis (see page 51), to which she may have belonged. There has also been a suggestion that she came from a wealthy family and even that she was the consort or wife of Jesus. These incredible theories have come from perusal of the ancient texts known as theNag Hammadi Scrolls.

THE NAG HAMMADI SCROLLS

In 1945 an Egyptian peasant was digging forsabakh,the fertile soil created by the latrines of the early hermits who had lived in caves near the village of Nag Hammadi in Upper Egypt. Suddenly he came upon a large jar made of red earthenware. He smashed it and found inside fifty-two papyrus scrolls bound in leather. He took them home, where his mother burned some of them in the oven. Fortunately the rest were taken to the local priest and were spotted by a local historian, who alerted an expert in Cairo. Finally, after much difficulty and in-fighting amongst experts and governments, the texts were translated and have now become known to the general public.

The papyri are dated at 350-400 CE and are Coptic translations of even earlier Greek texts. The date of the earlier texts is uncertain; many of them are contemporary with the gospels, but some may be pre-Christian. The whole collection includes texts such as theGospel of Thomas,theGospel of Philip,theSecret Gospel of John,theGospel of Truth,and theGospel to the Egyptians(also called 'The Sacred Book of the Great Invisible Spirit'), as well as poems, myths, and instruction for the practice of Mystery religions. The existence of some of these texts was already known from the writings of Bishop Irenaeus, who was condemning heresies as early as the second century CE.

These gospels, denounced as heretical by the growing orthodoxy of the Early Church Fathers, contain sayings of Jesus which are either different from those in the biblical gospels, or which can be viewed differently because of the new context in which they are placed. In terms of the quest for the Holy Grail, there are two particularly radical conclusions that can be drawn from this material.

The first is the importance of Mary Magdalene, who is named as the 'companion' or 'partner' of Jesus, and who was sufficiently intimate with Jesus for him to kiss her on the mouth:

... the companion of the Saviour is Mary Magdalene. But Christ loved her more than all the disciples and used to kiss her often on her mouth. The rest of the disciples were offended by it... They said to him, 'Whydoyou love her more than all of us?' The Savior answered and said to them, 'WhydoI not love you as [I love] her?'

This quote is from theGospel of Philip,which also relates the rivalry that came about between Mary Magdalene and Peter. Peter did not believe that women were worthy to be full followers of Christ and therefore disputed Mary's claim to having been taught special knowledge orgnosis,by Jesus. But in theDialogue of the Savior she is praised as a visionary who has been selected by Christ for special teaching. She is described as the 'woman who knew the All'.

Several sayings to this effect among the Nag Hammadi texts link with an earlier scroll, one of four, discovered in Egypt in 1896. This was theGospel of Mary(Magdalene). It opens with the reaction of the disciples after Jesus's death. They are terrified for their own lives but Mary Magdalene reassures them of Christ's continual presence. The fact that she has already seen him accords with the account given in St Mark's Gospel, but in this gospel she tells them she has received further teaching from him in a vision. When the disciples dispute this she weeps and says to Peter:

'My brother Peter, whatdoyou think?Doyou think that I thought this up myself inmyheart?Doyou think I am lying about the Savior?' Levi answered and said to Peter, 'Peter, you have always been hot-tempered ... If the Savior made her worthy, who are you to reject her?' 9

This is the beginning of a rift between Peter and Mary which became a serious doctrinal schism in the early Church. Mary claims to have seen the risen Christ and received teachings from him in a vision received 'through the mind'. She is not talking about a physically risen Christ, but a spiritual presence.

A SPIRITUAL RESURRECTION

This brings us to the second great revelation of these so-calledGnostic Gospels.They state that not only Mary but also some of the disciples received secret teachings from Jesus to the effect that the idea of the resurrection of the body was a crude misunderstanding of spiritual truth. This rejection of the bodily resurrection of Christ was linked to the concept ofdualism,the split between the spiritual and the material, which formed the core belief of the great heresy calledGnosticism,espoused by a group of early Christians. By the time of the Crusades this heresy was still strongly active and its main adherents were known as the Cathars.

THE CATHARS

The Cathars were also sometimes called theAlbigensiansbecause they lived near the town of Albi in the Languedoc area of southern France. They were attracted to this area because it was known for its religious tolerance, being independent from France at the time. New intellectual and philosophical ideas were able to flourish there, and it was also the home of the new Courtly Love poetry of the troubadours.

Although the Cathars considered themselves Christians, they claimed to have a special understanding of Christianity. They followed the secret teachings of Jesus, which they said, were found in mystical experience, just as

Mary Magdalene described. They believed that whereas Jesus taught only in parables to the general mass of his followers, he taught a secret higher knowledge to his disciples which they passed on only to those who were ready to understand it.

There are accounts in several of the Gnostic Gospels of some of the disciples having mystical experiences. For example, in theApocryphon of John, John recounts how he was in 'great grief' after the Crucifixion:

Immediately ... the [heavens were opened, and the whole] creation [which is] under heaven shone, and [the world] was shaken. [I was afraid, and I] saw in the light [a child] ... while I looked he became like an old man. And he [changed his] form again, becoming like a servant ... I saw ... an image with multiple forms in the light ...JO

In such accounts Jesus manifests himself not in bodily form but as a luminous presence or in a series of transformations. The Cathars believed that truth was revealed in this way and that such experience was open to anyone. They rejected the idea that Christians needed priestly intervention or instruction from the Church. In fact, they rejected

Church-based Christianity, believing it had become corrupted and patriarchal.

Because Mary Magdalene was the first to receive direct experience of the secret teachings of Christ, she became a figurehead for the Gnostics. They also venerated the idea of the Divine Feminine, which they felt was lacking in orthodox Christianity. They prayed to both the Divine Father and the Divine Mother. Sometimes the Divine Mother was worshipped independently as 'the mystical, eternal Silence', and a secret mass was held in which the wine symbolized her blood.

The Cathars also identified the Divine Feminine with the Holy Spirit. There is evidence from the Gnostic Gospels that the Holy Spirit was at one time considered to be female. For example, in hisGospelPhilip indignantly refutes the idea that Mary could have become pregnant by the Holy Spirit. He says: 'Some say that Mary conceived by the Holy Spirit: they are mistaken, they do not realize what they say. When did a female ever conceive by a Iernale?"

The Cathars also linked the Divine Feminine principle with the ancient Greek concept ofSophta,the female spirit of wisdom. The opening of John's Gospel was their credo. They believed Wisdom was 'the Word', who was 'in the beginning' and was 'with God'. She was also the Spirit who 'moved on the face of the waters' to effect the Creation. As such she was the feminine principal that lay behind the Creator God and was, some believed, more powerful.

All in all, the Cathars, in their reverence for the feminine, their disbelief in a physical resurrection and their belief in knowledge through spiritual revelation rather than doctrine, were considered dangerous heretics by the Roman Catholic Church. They were especially dangerous because their beliefs were popular and posed a real threat to orthodox Christianity.

THE ALBIGENSIAN CRUSADE

In 1208 Pope Innocent III called for a huge army to fight against the heretical Cathars. Although they considered themselves fellow Christians, the Pope considered them as threatening as the Muslims. The Albigensian Crusade was treated in the same way as the other Crusades, with knights being offeredindulgences,or pardons, in return for their services. The area targeted was Languedoc and it was difficult for the crusading knights to distinguish orthodox Catholics from heretics because they were coexisting peacefully. The appalling command from the papal legate has become infamous. He said: 'Kill them all, God will recognize his own!' The result was a huge massacre of the population of southern France.

Last to fall was the great Cathar stronghold, the castle on the mountain at Montsegur, This had been deliberately fortified for the protection of the heretics and was also said to hold the 'Cathar Treasure'. In 1243 Montsegur was besieged by an army of ten thousand men, and finally fell. The site below it is famous for the rounding up and mass burning of more than two hundred devotees. It is know today as the 'Field of the Burned'.

After the fall of Montsegur, the treasure was collected up, but much of it was found to have gone. Tradition has it that during the siege four of theParfaits,orPeriecti,the leaders of the Cathar faith, had escaped by rope down the mountainside, taking the treasure with them. This treasure has excited much speculation. Many believe that the most important and holy item they possessed was the Holy Grail itself.

One theory as to how it might have come into their possession is that it was brought over by Mary Magdalene. A cult of the Magdalene grew up in that area of France, as is still evident from the number of churches dedicated to her. It seems feasible that if she took refuge there then the Cathars, who revered her, should become the possessors of her treasure.

ARTHURIAN LEGEND - A SECRET CODE?

At the time when the Cathars were flourishing, the Arthurian legends were becoming extremely popular. Although the Catholic Church Was suspicious of these stories they tolerated them because they inspired knights to join the Crusades. They were suspicious of them because, although Arthur purported to be Christian, his Celtic origins were everywhere apparent in the stories, not least in the number of Celtic hermits that abounded in independent chapels in the mysterious forests where the knights' prowess was tested. Moreover, these hermits were always urging the knights on in their solitary efforts at self-improvement, thus suggesting that salvation could be attained through personal effort. This ran counter to the Church's belief in salvation through faith and, in particular, to the importance of the Church's sacraments and the role of its priests.

The other worrying aspect of the Arthurian legends was their adherence to the ideal of Courtly Love. This strange phenomenon had suddenly arisen in the poetry of the troubadours who lived in the Languedoc. Many theories have been put forward for this extraordinary new idealism in which women were made into objects of worship and adoration. The chivalric code of the knights served this ideal and their highest task seemed to be the service of women.

One theory put forward for this sudden elevation of the feminine is that it was an encoded form of the secret Feminine Mysteries espoused by the heretical sects. Knights on crusade had come into contact with Eastern mysticism, especially that of theSuits,the heretical sect of orthodox Islam. It is well known that the Sufis' erotic love poetry was a coded form of worship of the

Divine Feminine principle, and the Courtly Love motif of troubadour poetry and Arthurian legend may have performed the same function.

A HOME FOR THE GRAIL

If this were the case then it would be entirely appropriate that the story of the Holy Grail should be linked to the Arthurian Cycle. Arthur's knights were already inspired to extremes of personal prowess by devotion to the Feminine, so for them to seek the Holy Grail, a symbol of the highest form of spirituality, seems a natural progression - especially if it represented the secret female aspect of the deity.

Also, some of the descriptions of the Grail given in the Arthurian stories are very suggestive of the mystical experiences of Christ described in the Gnostic Gospels. For example, the idea of a great light emanating from the Grail, or the form of a child in the Grail who then turns into a man, is reminiscent of the transformations reported by the Gnostic visionaries. Also in the Grail stories there is a report of Arthur himself seeing five different transformations of the

Grail. This is inPerlesvaus,the anonymous French account of the Grail, which is arguably one of the most mystical. By contrast Malory seems determined to show the contents of the Grail as the transubstantiated body of Christ. His description is heavy-handed, almost as if he is trying to refute the suggestions made in previous accounts.

THE CULT OF ISIS

If the Grail symbolizes the Feminine Mysteries espoused by the Cathars, and if they were skeptical of the bodily resurrection of Christ then, it has been argued, their beliefs might go back to pre- Christian goddess worship. The most obvious candidate for this would be Isis, the great Egyptian goddess who was also regarded as the female principle of Nature.

The central story enshrined in her religion was that of the death and resurrection of Osiris, her consort. After he was killed by his evil brother she restored him to life. His resurrection was ritualistic and connected with cyclical renewal, fertility and the changing seasons. It therefore represented a mystery, a hidden spiritual truth, rather than being an actual physical occurrence. This was akin to the way in which the Gnostics regarded the resurrection of Christ. Certainly at the time of Christ the cult of Isis was still very strong. It is thought that some of the rituals used by Christianity may have been taken from it. For example, baptism was used by adherents of Isis to symbolize the washing away of sins.

Isis, herself, being an Earth goddess, was symbolic of the rich black soil that lined the Nile. She was often portrayed as a black mother holding a baby. This baby was Horus, son of her husband Osiris whom she brought back to life. Isis became the most prominent deity of Egypt, revered for her powers in connection with the resurrection of Osiris. She demonstrated the force of feminine love in conquering the death of the masculine.

Notre Dame de Clermont-Perrand

THE BLACK MADONNA

The image of Isis as the black mother goddess holding her baby is believed to have prefigured the statues of the Virgin Mary with the child Jesus. The extraordinary proliferation of Black Madonna's in the south of France supports this idea. It is well known that shrines to the Virgin Mary or to the saints were erected on ancient pagan sites and even that the names of the ancient deities were Christianized, so it is feasible to conjecture that a former pagan goddess cult in which a black goddess or Dark Mother was venerated, might be transformed into a sanctuary for the worship of the Virgin and Child.

It is thought to be no accident that the Grail legends, the cult of the Magdalene and the cult of the Black Madonna all became prominent in the area of Languedoc at the same time. This elevation of the Feminine, especially in its dark and mysterious aspect, has been explained psychologically as a reaction to the suppression of the feminine principle in orthodox Christianity. The only image allowed by the Roman Church was the chaste image of the Virgin, who was elevated to such a height of perfection that she could not, like the pagan representations of the Goddess, embody dual aspects of personality.

In the figure of the Virgin Mary, therefore, the negative or dark side of the feminine deity was split off. The Black Madonna's, by contrast, are thought to be manifestations of the neglected negative aspect of the Divine Feminine. It was, of course, the dark side of the Feminine that contained the secret teachings, the hidden mysteries and the divine gnosis.

The connection between the Black Madonna and the Grail is shown in the legends by the appearance of the loathly damsel Cundrie, who is called the Black Woman inPeredur.Despite her horrific appearance, she is intimately connected with the mysteries of the Grail. Not only does she follow Perceval to Arthur's Court and influence him to attempt the quest a second time, she also guides him. In fact, he goes so far as to seek her out when embarking on the quest, as he realizes that only she can help him to attain his goal.

APPLICATION - HONOURING THE DARK GODDESS

I am black, but beautiful

O yedaughters of Jerusalem

Although banished, the Dark Goddess still has her place. She can even be found in the pages of the Old Testament's Song of Solomon. The ancient understanding of her was as the container of opposites such as death and life, male and female, creation and destruction. The Celts had their triple goddess with three aspects: maiden, mother and crone. Other ancient religions also acknowledged and honored the different types of the feminine deity. Only the Christian religion split her in two, finding her dark face unacceptable. But still she returns, as the Black Madonna or, more dangerously, as an angry, destructive sorceress or witch.

The dark aspect of the Goddess symbolizes destruction, chaos, and death. In Jungian terms, un-integrated with her bright side, she can become uncontrollable. Her wise worshippers of old knew how to honor her in all her guises and to preserve her unity. But for the last millennium there has been a widespread dishonoring of women and female powers. Today, at a psychological level, and also at a spiritual one, there is a dawning realization that in the dishonoring of women through fear of their dark side, something of crucial importance has been lost.

This is what the Goddess, be she Isls, Sophia or one of the other myriad ancient female deities, has said about herself in one of the Gnostic Gospels. Ponder on it. Allow her dark face as well as her bright one to give you wisdom, her counsel to give you insight. Then explore her nature further by composing your own poem or creative work in her honor.

For it is|who am the first: and the last.

It is|who am the revered: and the despised.

It is|who am the harlot: and the holy.

It is|who am the wife: and the virgin.

It is|who am the mother: and the daughter ...

It is|who am the barren: and who has many children.

It is|who am the one whose marriage is magnificent: and who have not married.

It is|who am the midwife: and she who does not give birth ...

It is|who am the bride: and the bridegroom ...

And may those who have not recognized me become acquainted withme.

Chapter 7: The Templars Grail

Flegetanis knew the starry script

could readinthe heavens high

How the stars rollontheir courses,

how they circle the silent sky

And the time when the wandering endeth

- and the life and the lot of men

Heread in the stars, and strange secrets he saw.

THE KINGHTS TEMPLAR

When the Albigensian Crusade was launched by the Roman Catholic Church (see Chapter 5), there was one group of knights who refused to take part. These were the Knights Templars. This intriguing secret order seems to have had a close affinity with the Cathars. Indeed there are some who believe that at the time of the great massacre of Cathars some members of the sect smuggled the Holy

Grail out of Montsegur and passed it to the Templars.

The Seal of the Knights Templars

Certainly the Knights Templars have always been strongly linked with the Holy Grail. In fact, they have even been called the Keepers of the Grail. But who they were exactly, what their real purpose was, and where the extraordinary power they wielded at the time of the Crusades came from, are questions shrouded in mystery.

MYSTERIOUS ORIGINS

Around 1119, nine French noblemen led by a certain Hughes de Payens went to the King of Jerusalem and asked permission to form an order of Poor Knights, or warrior monks, whose function would be to serve in the Holy Land. Permission was granted and they were established in the Al-Aqsa Mosque on the site of the former Temple of Solomon (destroyed by the Romans in 68 CE). It was from this temple that they got their name.

Strangely, although their alleged purpose was to protect pilgrims, for nine years they did not increase their numbers but remained on the Temple site in Jerusalem. So it was not until 1128 that they were given official recognition at the Council of Troyes. It was also at this time that St Bernard of Clairvaux, founder of the Cistercian Order, wrote their Rule.

Being a monkish order the Templars had to adhere to the three vows of poverty, chastity and obedience. They were therefore not allowed to marry and no women were permitted to join the order. They wore white robes to which they later added the distinctive red cross pattee- a Celtic, or equal-armed, cross with splayed ends, which was also emblazoned on their shields.

AN INFLUENTIAL FORCE

After 1128 the Templars dramatically increased their numbers and, at the same time, started becoming extremely wealthy. Money was raised to fund their order and they also acquired lands and castles from the noblemen who joined them. Using their castles as strongholds, they became the bankers for the Crusades. They gained great respect and were even consulted by Kings. They were also granted privileges by the

Pope, including tax exemption. In the end they obtained such financial and religious freedom that they became a law unto themselves.

FREE THINKERS

The result of all this was that the Templars were able to enjoy independence of thought. They were not dominated by the orthodox teaching of the Roman Catholic Church, and at the same time they were exposed to the sophistication of Eastern philosophy. Many of them learned Arabic or employed Arabic secretaries and discovered that the 'infidels' were in many ways more learned and civilized than the Christians.

The freedom of exchange of information enjoyed by the Templars meant that they were able to bring back to the West important new ideas in medicine, masonry and architecture. They also investigated the mathematical, astronomical, philosophical and religious learning of the East. At the same time they amply fulfilled their stated purpose. They were an extremely disciplined force of proud and brave warriors who were prepared to fight to the death to support the cause of the Crusades.

Although the Crusades began well, with the Christian armies initially capturing Jerusalem, their position gradually worsened over the years. While the enemy had been divided within itself between Muslim and Mongol forces, the Christians had enjoyed the advantage, but when the Muslims defeated the Mongols and were then joined by the Mamluks, the Christian cause became increasingly hopeless. After a long struggle SaladIn, King of Egypt, captured Jerusalem in 1187 and the Templars were forced out of the city, moving their headquarters to Cyprus. The Crusades continued for another hundred years but after the siege of Acre in 1291 they were effectively over.

With the ending of the wars the purpose of the Templars was apparently gone, but they remained as an independent secret society, swearing allegiance to one another rather than to any king or country. Rumors grew up around them suggesting that they now had some other purpose, perhaps involving some kind of secret knowledge or information.

STRANGE RITUALS

Although they had commanded such respect during the Crusades, it is easy to see why the Templars became discredited. Although it was not their fault, they were criticized for the loss of Jerusalem. They were also accused of collaborating with the enemy in order to protect their wealth. Much of this criticism came from fear and jealousy. Their wealth and independence must have made them seem very threatening. Rumors arose concerning strange rituals performed in their secret initiation ceremonies. These included worshipping cats, Satanic idols and mysterious heads, killing babies, eating the ashes of dead Templars and spitting on images of the Cross. They were also believed to be magicians, alchemists and occultists and, as such, were accused of practicing witchcraft and supporting heretical beliefs.

PERSECUTION OF THE TEMPLARS

With the declared aim of purifying France of heresies - but probably because he needed money - Philip IV of France sent hundreds of his agents out on Friday 13 October and arrested the French Templars en masse, with no prior warning. These arrests were actually illegal but the Pope owed his position to Philip so had no choice but to side with him. With the Pope's support, other raids were made across Europe and the Templars were put on trial.

The charges laid against them hinged on their alleged denial of the Crucifixion. Under extreme torture, confessions were obtained that supported these charges as well as some of the strange rumors. For an order which had been highly respected as upholders of Christianity, these admissions were shocking. Even so, nothing

could be proved conclusively against them and as a result no final verdict was ever reached. Nevertheless, as a result of Philip bullying the Pope, the entire order was officially dissolved in March 1312.

THE CURSE OF THE TEMPLARS

Two years later, the Grand Master of the Templars, Jacques de Molay, was sentenced to life imprisonment, having also confessed to iniquitous practices. But instead of accepting his sentence, at the last minute he retracted his confession saying that his only sin was that of lying under torture and admitting to 'the disgusting charges laid against the Order'. He declared that the Order was innocent, 'its purity and saintliness' beyond question. He ended by stating that because life was offered to him only 'at the price of infamy', it was not worth having.

Accordingly, Jacques de Molay was condemned to death and was burned alive along with Geoffrey de Charnay, the Preceptor of Normandy, outside the Cathedral of Notre Dame. Before he died, de Molay cursed Phi lip of France and the Pope for their crimes against the Templars, calling for their reckoning within a year. Within the year both were dead.

TREASURES OF THE TEMPLARS

After their dissolution, the mystique of the Templars persisted, not least because of the disappearance of their treasure. If Philip IV was hoping to get his hands on it he was disappointed. After the trials surprisingly little of it was found, but this was given by the Pope to the Order of the Knights Hospitallers. So what had happened to the rest of it? Some believe that despite the suddenness of Philip's arrests, word had leaked out just in time for some of the Templars to set sail from the west coast of France, where their fleet was moored, and take their most important treasures elsewhere. Naturally, if it were in their keeping, their chief treasure would have been the Holy Grail itself.

The idea that the Templars were the guardians of the Grail has always been a strong one, not least because it is supported in two important Grail texts. These lie slightly outside the main Grail canon because they were not directly used by Malory. They are the anonymous FrenchPerlesvausand the GermanParzival.

THE TEMPLARS AS A MYSTICAL SECT IN PERLESVAUS

This lively account, also calledThe High History of the Grail,contains such knowledgeable and detailed descriptions of battle that some have suggested it may have actually been written by a Templar. It also contains two passages, which seem to relate directly to the Templars.

One is when Perceval is taken by magic ship to an island where he comes across two masters and thirty-three men in white robes, which bear red crosses. These would appear to be initiates of some sort and they are certainly wearing the Templar costume. They tell him about a quantity of heads sealed in lead, silver and gold, and more specifically, of the head of a king and a queen. These sealed heads strongly suggest both alchemy and the cult of the severed head, which goes back to the Celtic god Bran, but they are also linked with the secret rituals of the Templars. The second passage is when a priest is depicted as defiling the Cross by hitting it. This is similar to the confessions extracted from the Templars under torture.

It also reflects the Catharist contempt for the Crucifixion, which is one reason why many think the Cathars and the Templars were closely linked. This idea seems to be confirmed by the fact that the names of several Cathar nobles were found on the Templars' roll of members. Added to this the text of the Perlesvausis mystical and in places appears to support Gnostic ideas. One example is when Arthur witnesses the Mass of the Virgin, and also five 'changes of the

Grail'. There is also a battle between the Fisher King and his brother, the King of Castle Mortal, symbolic of the battle between the flesh and the spirit.

THE TEMPLARS IN PARZIVAL

Although the connection between the Templars and the Grail is only speculative in thePerlesvaus,the text that unquestionably links the two isParzival,a bold and exuberant version of the Grail story written by the German author Wolfram von Eschenbach around 1200 CE. The nature of the Grail was in debate even at that time, and Wolfram depicts it as a sacred stone. He also claimed that Chretien de Troyes was ignorant of the real meaning of the 'Gral', but that he himself had received the true story from 'Kyot the Provencale'. Some scholars believe Kyot is a fictional character, but others have identified him as Guiot of Provence, a troubadour and possibly a Templar initiate.

In Wolfram's text the Templars are specifically named as guardians of the Grail. They are the chosen ones who are nourished by it and who guard it on Munsalvaesche, the Mount of Salvation. He says:

".. .many formidable fighting-men dwell at Munsalvaesche with the Gral. They are continually riding out on sorties in quest of adventure. Whether these same Templars reap trouble or renown, they bear it for their sins. A warlike company lives there. I will tell you how they are nourished. They live from a Stone whose essence is most pure. If you have never heard of it I shall name it for you here. It is called 'Lapstt exillts'. By virtue of this Stone the Phoenix is burned to ashes, in which he is reborn. Thus does the Phoenix moult its feathers! Which done, it shines dazzling bright and lovely as before!... This Stone is also called 'The Gral'."

The term lapsit exillis has puzzled many scholars. Some read it as lapsit ex caelis, a stone falling from the heavens, others identify it as lapis elixir, the alchemical Philosopher's Stone which 'turned all to gold'. Alchemists believed that this stone had healing properties and could also bestow eternal life and youth on the possessor. Certainly the image of the phoenix rising from its ashes is a familiar one in alchemy. In his actual description of the Grail procession, however, Wolfram is more allusive. He speaks of a large translucent stone which is carried in front of the Grail. The Grail itself he does not describe, except to say that it is 'the consummation of heart's desire, its root and blossoming ... paradisal, transcending all earthly perfection'." It is carried by the Princess of the Grail family, who wears a dress of Arabian silk. Her name is given as Repanse de Schoye (Chosen Response).

EASTERN ORIGINS

The alchemical associations hinted at in this passage and elsewhere have given rise to the idea that the Grail represents the Hermetic Vessel used in alchemy. But besides alchemy, Wolfram'sParzivalalso contains allusions to other Eastern spiritual sciences such as astrology, astronomy, and the Kabbala. Added to this, half-way through the text he breaks off to announce that Kyot, the man who told him the tale, found it in Toledo in an Arabic script.

This script had originally been written long before the birth of Christ by a Jew named Flegetanis who was descended from Solomon . Flegetanis was an astronomer who discovered the Grail in the secrets of the stars. He declared that spiritual beings brought it to earth and withdrew again. Afterwards it came into the care of a body of worthy Christians 'bred to a pure life'. On hearing this story Kyot went looking for the men who were custodians of the Grail and found them in France.

This further reference to the Templars is followed by a reminder that in this Grail account Parzival's mother is a dark-skinned Eastern queen. Parzival also has a piebald younger half-brother named Feirefiz whom he has never met. At the end of the story they fight each other without realizing they are related. Fortunately they discover each other's identity before either is killed. After this, Cundrie the sorceress reappears and addresses Feirefiz in Christian terms and Parzival in astronomical ones. She asks their forgiveness and offers to make amends for her former anger. Then the two brothers set out to achieve the Grail together. Parzival asks the question and becomes the next Grail King with Condwiramors (Blancheflor in Chretien's story) as his queen. Although Feirefiz is at first unable to see the Grail because he has not been baptized, this is put right and he ends up actually marrying the Grail Maiden, Repanse de Schoye. (From this unexpected liaison the enigmatic Prester John is born; see Chapter 7.)

The fact that Wolfram gives the name Chosen Response to the Grail Maiden suggests that he is concerned to unite heathen and Christian through their response to the Grail. In this he may be reflecting the attitude of the Templars themselves. Although they were fierce and faithful fighters, they began to respect and adopt Eastern wisdom and learning. It is even possible that the germ of the Grail story came from the East and was brought to Europe by the Templars, as well as the Grail itself.

APPLICATION - THE WISDOM OF THE ALCHEMY

Jung considered that alchemy formed a link between the Gnostics and twentieth-century depth psychology. Although alchemy has been discredited by charlatan practitioners who tried to use it as a means of making gold, the true alchemist considered his work to be a bridge between the earthly and spiritual planes. The questor might find that an appreciation of the fundamental philosophy of alchemy leads to a deeper understanding of the Grail mysteries.

Wolfram von Eschenbach describes the Grail as a stone with magical properties. This has been thought to refer to the Philosophers' Stone whichwas saidto turn base matter into gold. This is allegorical as much as chemical, the gold symbolizing the final transformation of matter into spirit.

The process by which this was thought to be attainedis an extremely skilled and complex one. First themateria prima,or base material, has to be mixed with the First Agent, or secret fire. Both have to be prepared and purified before they can be mixed together. One represents the feminine principle of mercury, the other the masculine sulphuric principle. The two materials are then enclosed in the Philosophic Egg, a hermetically sealed vessel which is activated by a constant interrnal heat. The materials interact, at first corrupting each other, which is described as a death. This is followed by etprocess of decay and corruption and issues in the black liquidnigredo.This phase eventually ends when a starry aspect appears, caused by the properties of mercury reasserting themselves.

An intensification of heat applied at this time gives rise to a beautiful array of colours called the Peacock's Tail, which symbolizes resurrection. The colours eventually blend into a whiteness called albedo. But this is not the end. The albedo undergoes a strengthening process and turns red. This stage is known as the Red King or the Red Rose. Eventually the whole 'work' produces the Philosophers' Stone.

From this brief account it can be seen that the Holy Grail, although depicted as a stone in Parzival and in this way made symbolic of the alchemical process, can also in its more usual chalice shape represent the Hermetic Vessel which contained the Materia Prima. The spear would then represent the masculine principle of the secret fire. The two interacting together chemically undergo a symbolic death and resurrection, emerging in a transcendent form.

The deep truths that alchemy seeks to represent cannot be found in linear or logical thinking. Like the Grail itself, its language is symbolic. An insight into the secret knowledge of alchemy can be gained by a contemplation of some of its many detailed pictures or engravings. Often these depict the different stages of the 'work'.

Relax and clear your mind of all logical or intellectual thinking. Contemplate the picture below and let the symbols speak to your unconscious self.

The Mercury of the Philosophers

Chapter 8: Symbolism Of The Grail

All questors are aware of the significance of the symbolism £"\surrounding the Grail. This extends to the objects, colors, landscape and people connected with it. This chapter offers some clues to a greater understanding of that symbolism. It can also be regarded as a useful consolidation of information from previous chapters.

THE FOUR ELEMENTS

The importance of these has been examined in Chapter 2 in relation to the four great treasures of the Celts. The theory of the Four Elements underlies all later philosophical, alchemical, scientific and mystical thinking. It was accepted by the three great religions - Christianity, Islam and Judaisrn - and an attempt was made to unite them on this basis.

THE SPEAR

The spear was originally the Spear of Lightning and one of the four Celtic Hallows. It later became identified with the lance with which the centurion Longinus pierced Christ's side while on the Cross, releasing blood and water which were caught in the Grail Chalice by joseph of Arimathea. It was also the lance, which Balin used to deal the Dolorous Stroke and maim King Pelles. During the First Crusade it was supposedly discovered at Antioch after a monk was told of its whereabouts in a dream. Its discovery heartened the Christians and helped them achieve victory in this Crusade. After this it became a sacred relic. Hitler later became obsessed with this relic, believing it bestowed invincibility on its owner.

Symbolically the spear denotes masculinity. In connection with the Grail it is seen as a symbol of male fertility. It is related to the rays of the sun and therefore of fire, and symbolizes the action of Being on Matter. The drops of blood dripping from the spear, if introduced into the Grail, regenerate the Matter within it. In the Grail legend the spear is the instrument both of affliction and of healing.

THE ROUND TABLE

The Round Table was Guinevere's marriage gift to Arthur, and previously belonged to her father. Originally, however, Merlin made it for Arthur's father, King Uther. It arrived with a hundred knights. Arthur was delighted and appointed Merlin to choose a further fifty knights for it. The names of the chosen knights appeared in gold letters over the seats, but at that time two were left empty. The Round Table symbolized the round world and cosmic order. The breaking up of it, which Arthur foresaw at the outset of the Grail quest, brought disharmony and disorder to the kingdom.

The Round Table is inextricably connected with the Grail legends, not least because the Holy Grail first appears in the middle of it in order to provoke the Quest for its mysteries. But there is an account, which connects the Round Table even more directly to the Grail. Robert de Boron says that Joseph of Arimathea was inspired by the Holy Spirit to set up a Table of the Grail modeledon the Table of the Last Supper. Because Judas left early to betray Jesus, a place was always left empty at the Grail Table. This table was in turn the model for the Round Table, and Judas's seat became theSiege Perilous,or Dangerous Seat, that could only be occupied by the perfect hero. According to Malory, the Round table held 150 knights, the same number as went on the Grail quest.

GWENDDOLAU'S CHESSBOARD

This is a magic chessboard, one of the Thirteen Treasures of Britain, guarded by Merlin. It belonged to the pagan King Gwenddolau, who was killed in a great battle with a Christian King. His board was said to be extremely beautiful, made of gold and silver. It was mystical in that the pieces could play by themselves. Perceval plays against them inPeredur.He loses and throws the board into a lake in anger. He later has to recover it under the direction of the Black Woman. Gawain also encounters this chessboard, on one occasion using it as a shield. In Celtic myth this board game was calledgwyddbwyll,orfidchellin Ireland.

Chess also has oriental origins. It came to Spain and France via the Arabs, who respected it on two levels. It offered valuable training in terms of military strategy, and possessed mystical and symbolic properties. For example, the Queen is the most powerful piece. She can move in any direction and can overcome any opponent. She is nothing less than the Empress of the Board, having the same powers as all the other pieces except the knights. The board itself is thought to symbolize the land. InPeredurthe chessboard is under the protection of the Black Lady but belongs to the Empress.

This magical board is a persistent motif in both the Arthurian and the Grail legends.

THE FISHER KING

The Fisher King was the guardian of the Grail. The fish was an ancient symbol of spirituality. The Celts believed that the oldest and wisest creature was the Salmon of Knowledge that lived at the bottom of the Well of Wisdom. Anyone lucky enough to catch and eat it would be imbued with wisdom and prophetic powers. The fish also symbolized life and fertility. It became the symbol for Christ, the Greek letters inIchthus(Fish) being also the chief Greek letters forJesus Christ God's Son Saviour.The symbol of the fish was therefore widely used by the early Christians. Christ was also known as the Fisher of Men. The Fisher King could therefore be seen as an ancient King of wisdom and fertility and also as Christ.

In one of the Grail stories an attempt is made to explain the Fisher King. He is said to be Brons, brother-in-law to Joseph of

Arimathea, and to have caught a single fish, which fed all the Grail company. The name Brons also suggests a link to the Celtic god Bran (see Chapter 2). In yet another account the Fisher King is Joseph of Arimathea himself. Elsewhere he is known as King Pelles, or Pellam. He is sometimes identified with the Maimed King who languishes from a wound in the thighs, or genitals, which also causes barrenness in the land.

PELLES OR PELLAM (SEE ALSO THE FISHER KING, ABOVE)

Pelles is King of Corbenic, the Grail Castle. He is father of Elaine, the Grail bearer, and connives in her plot to seduce Lancelot. He is also the one to receive the Dolorous Stroke from Balin. In some accounts Pelles is the son of Pellam. In others, the two are confused.

GARLON

Garlon is the brother of King Pelles. He is the invisible knight, also called black-faced. Symbolically he is the unconscious shadow-side of the King. The black magician, Clinschor (or K1ingsor) inParzival,is also thought to be linkedto him, as is the King of Castle Mortal who is brother to the Fisher King in thePerlesvaus.

THE WASTE LAND

This was the land ruled over by the Fisher King, also sometimes called the Maimed King. The land was laid waste by the Dolorous Stroke which rendered the King infertile. Both would be healed when the Grail hero appeared and asked the correct question. The implication is that the land was once paradisal and now needs a hero to restore it. The Land is linked to the Sovereign in Celtic myth. The Sovereign needs a healthy King or consort in order to regenerate the land. In the Grail legends the Waste Land suffers from sterility on both a physical and spiritual level. Spiritual sterility occurs when religion becomes devoid of feeling or direct experience. This parched land awaits the hero who will 'free the waters', and release the feminine powers of regeneration.

THE CASTLE Of CORBENIC

This is the Grail Castle. Corben means crow, so the castle has been identified with Dinas Bran, also known as Crow Castle, near L1angollen in Wales. Both the location and the link with the god Bran are suggestive in this respect. In the legends the Grail Castle mysteriously appears and disappears but before the rape of the Damsels of the Wells it was always visible. Symbolically, therefore, it is related to the powers of the feminine and to the land.

THE GRAIL MAIDEN

Elaine, the daughter of King Pelles, is the usual bearer of the Grail. Together with the powerful sorceress Dame Brisen, and with the connivance of her father, she tricks Lancelot into fathering Galahad by her. Instead of being angry, Lancelot recognizes that she is possessed of unusual wisdom. She is, therefore, the wise mother of the Grail hero.

In almost all accounts the Grail bearer is female. She is linked to the Damsels of the Wells who once offered drinks in golden cups to travelling knights. She is guardian of the Water of Life. In Wolfram's *Parzival* the Grail bearer is an Eastern Princess named Repanse de Schoye, or Chosen Response. This brings her to a point of identification with the Grail itself.

FEIREFIZ

In Wolfram's *Parzival* Feirefiz is Parzival's half-brother. He is 'dazzlingly elegant' but also piebald, being the offspring of a black Eastern Queen and a white father. He is a noble hero because of his service of Love. He is the heathen brother to the Christian hero. He makes the correct response to the Grail Maiden and marries her. His mottled skin may symbolize the dualism inherent in the Catharist faith, as well as the mingling of East and West.

PRESTER JOHN

Wolfram says Prester John was the offspring of Feirefiz and Repanse de Schoye, and thus cousin to Arthur, This was a bold stroke to explain a strange character.

In 1145 rumours began circulating of a rich and powerful Christian King who ruled a country somewhere near India. In 1165 letters were received by top potentates in the West from this same King, calling himself 'John, priest by the Almighty power of God' and assuring them of his extensive lands and wealth and of the Christianity of his kingdom. The Crusaders were heartened by news of such a monarch who would be a powerful ally in their cause. However, his identity was never ascertained. Marco Polo claimed to have met a monarch bearing the same title. Others say he was Genghis

Khan. He is also said to be linked with the Nestorian Church. Another theory is that he was descended from the Magi. He remains a mysterious figure and some Grail seekers have claimed him on an inner level as a Grail keeper for today.

THE SHIP OF SOLOMON

And had he set the sail, or had the boat
Become a living creature clad with wings?

This is the ship on which the three Grail heroes sail, guided by Dindrane, Perceval's sister. They find an extraordinary bed on it which is made from the Tree of Life and which once belonged to King Solomon. On the bed is the half-drawn sword of David. Dindrane makes new girdles for the sword (see Chapter 4).

Several ships feature in the final stages of the Grail quest. Lancelot and Galahad spend six months on one, and Dindrane is found lying dead in another. They symbolize the means of transportation from this world to that of the spirit. Perceval is taken to several islands, which are reminiscent of the Celtic Otherworld.

SARRAS

This is the 'holy' city where the three main Grail heroes finally arrive, directed there by Christ in order to receive a fuller experience of the powers of the Grail. It is the place where Galahad is made King and rules for a year. Both Galahad and Dindrane are buried there and, in one account, Perceval is too. It is thought to be located somewhere on the borders of Egypt. Even though it is a pagan city, it is called holy in the texts. The fact that the Grail has to go to the East to be fully experienced suggests an acknowledgement of the importance of Eastern religious thinking.

THE GRAIL CHAPEL

This is another place where the Grail can be witnessed. But in this setting it is stripped of some of its Celtic accouterments, such as the procession, the feast and the company. The Grail chapel offers a pared-down, more obviously Christian experience. It is presided over by a hermit rather than a king. However, it is often used to give a foretaste of the final Grail experience; for example, when Lancelot sees a wounded knight being healed, presumably in token of the Maimed King's experience (See Chapter 4).

In general, the Grail chapel offers a welcome oasis of light in the middle of a dark place. It is located either in a deep forest or, in the case of the Perilous Chapel, in a dark and fearful cemetery haunted by ghostly black knights. There is another chapel of this kind inPerlesvausin which Arthur and his knights have to fight off black knights who turn into demons until the chapel can be exorcized and sanctified again.

HERMITS

The hermits maintain the holiness and sanctuary of the chapels. They provide places of healing for wounded knights and also act as spiritual advisers to questing knights. They can also be seen as the last guardians of Celtic Christian belief. In Parzival the hermit Trevrizant is brother to the Fisher King and therefore related to Joseph of Arimathea. The most prominent Grail hermit, Nacien, presumed to look too closely into the Grail and was blinded. His sight was restored by three drops of blood from the lance. This shows that the hermit, although a wise guide, is not the Grail hero and therefore does not have the right to experience the Grail fully.

SAINT BERNARD OF CLAIRVAUX

Founder of the Order of Cistercian monks. He also wrote the Rule for the Order of Knights Templars. A very charismatic man, he inspired the second crusade with his preaching. As a child he had been taken to see the Black Virgin of Chatillon and received the miraculous grace - three drops of milk issuing from her breast. He was profoundly affected by this. As a consequence, the huge numbers of abbeys built by his Order were all dedicated to the Virgin Mary. He wrote 300 sermons on the Song of Songs and generally promoted veneration of the female through his adoration of the Virgin Mary. The Cistercian Order was instrumental in promoting the Arthurian legends, especially that of the Grail, in theVulgate Cycle,their vast compilation of Arthurian literature.

THE CAILLEACH

Originally an ancient Celtic goddess and Earth Mother. She is the Hag of Winter and often has a blue face. As the seasons change she becomes younger and more beautiful. She is also the Hag of Beare or the Dark Lady, being the dark face of Sovereignty, the Queen of the land. She often appears in her hag-like guise and tests the hero, usually demanding a kiss or a more binding demonstration of love before revealing her true beauty. The Loathly Lady whom Gawain was obliged to marry was a type of Cailleach. She turned into a beautiful woman when he had pledged himself to her and acknowledged her sovereignty. The Cailleach challenges all who enter the Grail quest. The gift of discernment is important in dealing with her. Apparent beauty or ugliness can be deceptive. She is the bestower of wisdom and the gift of kingship.

THE CASTLE OF MAIDENS

In Welsh tradition the Castle of Maidens was located at Gloucester, and in Scottish tradition, at Edinburgh. In theVulgate Cycle Galahad comes upon it by the River Severn. He rescues the maidens inside by killing the seven knights who hold them prisoner. Allegorically they have been considered to be the Seven Deadly Sins and the castle to be Hell. Galahad's mission is a re-enactment of the descent of Christ into Hell to release the souls of the righteous, which here are represented by the Maidens.

Another version of the Castle of Maidens is found underwater. An example is the underwater palace where Lancelot is brought up by the Lady of the Lake. This is also a type of Otherworldly Island. In Celtic myth a hero could be lured away to such a place by a beautiful maiden. Castles, walled towns, enclosed gardens and underwater islands are all aspects of the Otherworld, which can be seen as a realm where great treasures are located. It is also a place of enchantment from which it is almost impossible to escape. Heroes who enter are tempted to stay and risk losing their fighting prowess.

In Arthurian legend there are many other Castles containing Maidens that appear to be in genuine distress. These are all versions of the Castle of the Maidens found by Galahad. But in these other castles the hero is lured inside and imprisoned by the maidens. This happens with Lancelot and Morgan le Fey, and to

Bors, who is entertained in a castle and tempted sexually by its Lady.

The Maidens of the castle are often faery beings, enchantresses or sorcerers as well as hapless women in need of rescuing. Psychologically they are symbols of theanima,the feminine aspect or soul of a man. The anima has both positive and negative aspects and it is the hero's task to rescue and transform his own 'inner feminine'.

THE NUMBER NINE

Nine is the mystical number associated with women in the Grail legends. The Celts had a high regard for the number as their goddesses were often depicted in threes, symbolizing the mother, maiden and crone motif. Three times three being nine, this number was especially powerful. In Celtic legend to go beyond the ninth wave was to go beyond the known land, perhaps to where the Otherworld began.

Nine was especially associated with companies of mysterious women. The cauldron, which was kept in the Otherworldly realm of Annwn, was warmed by the breath of nine priestesses. There are correspondingly nine witches whom Arthur and his men kill at the end ofPeredur.(They are numbered in the story). There were nine druidesses on the Isle de Sein who tended the souls of the dead. There were also nine orders of angels according to esoteric Christianity and, in Greek mythology, nine muses.

APPLICATION - USING THE TAROT

Some truths are too deep to be expressed in words. They can be understood better in the form of symbols. The Cathars knew this and it is thought by some that they created the Tarot as a symbolic form of their beliefs. (TheMarseillesdeck is considered one of the oldest.) Certainly the figures of the Hermit, the Magician and the Pope suggest this.

Some of the older decks have been reproduced and their symbolism is obviously closer to the original meanings.

At the same time, their imagery is often very detailed and will repay study. There are also many modern and imaginative decks, which honour the ancient wisdom of the cards.

The Tarot should never be used as a cheap fortune-telling game; it is intended as a gateway to a deeper understanding of spiritual truths. Listed below are some of the images in the Major Arcana, with suggestions as to their Catharist meanings. A reappraisal of the Tarot in this light will make using it a richer experience and will link it to the symbolic language of the Grail. Instead of a spread, try using a single-card reading. This will help you focus more fully on some of the deeper meanings involved.

The Fool represents the seeker after inner knowledge.

The Magician, like the Alchemist, represents the inner process of transformation.

The High Priestess - is the mystical feminine principle of wisdom and insight.

The Empress - represents female sovereignty and motherhood.

The Hierophant - is Pope or Initiator. Represents religious doctrine.

The Lovers - are the highest union of male and female, leading to transformation.

The Hermit -is a wise guide and understands the loneliness of the spiritual quest.

The Hanged Man -offers a different perspective, a more intuitive spirituality.

Death-denotes great change, preparation/for a new emotional or spiritual beginning.

The Hanged Man

Temperance -is the Grail Maiden pouring out the Water of Life, creating balance.

The Devil -is the Magician in reverse, misusing power egotistically.

TheTower - denotes a breaking free from old constraints of habits or beliefs.

The Moon -is the unconscious, the female energies of the earth, the dark mother.

The Sun -is conscious masculine energy, achievement and satisfaction.

The World -is wholeness, synthesis, transcendence and completion.

Chapter 9: The Quest Continues

For allmyblood dancedin me, and I knew

That I should light upon the Holy Grail.

Down the centuries there has been continual speculation concerning the Grail. Interest in it became particularly strong in the nineteenth century when writers and artists, most notably Tennyson and the Pre-Raphaelites, returned to the Arthurian legends for inspiration. In the main they based their work on Malory's Morte d'Arthur, which had long been considered the classic text. Nevertheless, Tennyson in his great work Idylls of the King moved away from Malory when he came to write the section on the Holy Grail. Here hechose to follow the 'real man'Percivale,rather than the idealized Galahad of Malory's story.

Tennyson's poem cuts deep because he seems to be undecided as to whether the quest of the Grail is a glorious or an illusory one. In it Arthur warns his knights that they may be following 'wandering fires' rather than achieving helpful deeds of chivalry. His kingdom suffers from the effects of so many knights leaving to go on the quest and the poem ends with Arthur questioning the nature of spiritual vision.

While Tennyson was writing his Idylls, Wagner was composing his opera Parsifal. Not surprisingly, this was inspired by Wolfram von Eschenbach's German text, Parzival. Since then artists and Grail- seekers have increasingly moved towards this more mystical and esoteric text. This is because it is informative on a physical as well as a spiritual level. By associating it firmly with the Templars, Wolfram provided a strong historical starting-point for seekers of the Grail as a physical artifact. Not all seekers, however, were inspired by the highest motives.

HITLER'S ABORTIVE QUEST

Directly inspired by Wagner's opera, Adolph Hitler was one of the first to attempt to find the physical Grail. He had already acquired a relic thought to be the Lance of Longinus, whichwas found at Antioch in the First Crusade, and which he believed gave him unearthly power. Now he wanted the Grail itself. He sent Otto Rahn to the Cathar stronghold of Montsegur to search the numerous caves below the mountain for the Grail, which Rahn believed was the emerald stone that had fallen to earth from Lucifer's crown, as suggested inParzival.Rahn became obsessed, using geomancy and hermetic theories in his search but he was ultimately unsuccessful.

Rudolf Hess, the deputy Nazi leader, is also thought to have been sent after the Grail by Hitler, this time to Rosslyn Chapel near Edinburgh. Hess defected while on his quest and Hitler retaliated by sending many Freemasons and astrologers to concentration camps. Later he sent a further team to Montsegur in a last desperate attempt to find the Grail, believing its powers would prevent the re-conquest of France by the Allies. But this quest for the Grail as a source of unholy power failed.

THE GRAIL AS BLOODLINE

The German mystic and founder of Anthroposophy, Rudolph Steiner, was also drawn to the Grail legends. He distinguished between exoteric or outward Christianity (that of the Church) and esoteric Christianity, an inner wisdom which ran back through mystical societies like the Theosophists, the Rosicrucians and the Freemasons to the Templars and the Cathars. He was drawn to the European and Nordic mysteries rather than to those of the East. His pupil Walter Stein wrote a book *World History in the Light of the Grail* in 1928 in which he came up with a curious but compelling new theory concerning the Grail. It is thought that ideas from this book may have been the inspiration behind the studies of Michael Baigent, Richard Leigh and Henry Lincoln, whose controversial book *The Holy Blood and the Holy Grail* exploded onto the world in 1982, provoking a new and passionate interest in the Grail.

In their book, the three authors put forward the theory that theSangrailorSangreal(an alternative term for the Grail) represented a royal bloodline and should be read asSang Real,Royal Blood. They claim that Jesus was a Nazarite (a member of an esoteric religious sect), that he married Mary Magdalene, and that the Holy Grail that she brought to France was in fact their child carried in her womb.

They further suggest that this bloodline became allied with the royal line of the Franks, giving rise to the extraordinary Merovingian dynasty of priest-kings, which ruled France in the fifth and sixth centuries. So sacred and magical was this line that the Pope made a pact with them, which was later broken with the assassination of Dagobert II in 679. Dagobert's son escaped to Languedoc and the authors suggest that his line continued there and ended in Godfroi de Bouillon, founder of the mysterious order, the Priory of Sion, which was closely connected to the Templars.

BENEATH THE TEMPLE OF SOLOMON

In fact the Templars seem to hold the key to all the recent speculations concerning the true nature of the Grail. The mysteries surrounding their secret rites and their guardianship of a sacred object are at the heart of it. We have already seen how they might have received the Holy Grail from the Cathars just before the fall of Montsegur (see Chapter 5), but there is another route by which they might have come to possess a sacred object.

As noted in Chapter 6, when the Templar Order was first formed, its nine members spent nine years on the site of the ancient Temple of Solomon, without increasing their numbers. If they were supposed to be guarding travelling pilgrims then they were hardly in a position to do so effectively. So what were they doing for those nine years? Some have suggested that they were searching the Temple Stables, a vast system of man-made vaults and corridors beneath the Temple, for a well-hidden treasure left there after the siege of Jerusalem in 70 CE. If they did find an important treasure, this could explain their sudden rise in wealth and status as well as the mystery that continued to surround them.

Whether they discovered something of great value in this way, or whether they were entrusted with a sacred treasure by the Cathars is still not known. Nevertheless many researchers now believe such a treasure exists and have begun speculating on its nature. Taking their clue from the Templars' strange rituals, they even believe they may finally be on its track. .

THE TEMPLARS MYSTERIES

Two of the most offensive confessions made by the Templars, albeit under torture, were that they worshipped an idol called Baphomet and that they required initiates to revile and spit on the Cross.

Baphomet has been described as a jeweled skull or a bearded human head. This description is based on the following entry in the list of charges made against them in 1308:

Being that in each province they had idols, namely heads. That they adored these idols, that theysaidthe head could save them. Thatitcould make riches, make the trees flower, and make the land germinate.

The idea of a head having the mystical property to cause the land to germinate harks back to the oldest account of the Grail story,Peredur,in which the revered object is a severed head on a dish. It also relates to the power of the Grail being able to restore health to the land. The motif of the severed head is a strong one in Arthurian legend. It begins with such famous beheadings as that inGawain and the Green Knightand extends through

Chretien to the 150 sealed heads inPerlesvaus.

In much of the recent speculation concerning the Grail, the idea of its being a head, or an image of a head, has been prominent. First the idea of its being the Head of Christ on the Turin Shroud was put forward, then the severed head of John the Baptist was suggested and, most recently, and most shockingly, Keith Laidler has made a leap from these suggestions to the idea that the Holy Grail is the actual mummified head of Christ, kept hidden down the centuries, but guarded and worshipped by a succession of secret sects, including the Templars.

He bases this astonishing claim not only on the confessions of the Templars but also on a Grail account which says that Nicodemus carved a likeness of Jesus's head that was so real it was 'as if God himself made it'. He puts this together with the fact that Nicodemus accompanied Joseph of Arimathea to Jesus's tomb and took with him a hundred pounds of spices, which must have been for embalming. Also, according to legend, Nicodemus was one of the company who sailed to France with Joseph of Arimathea and Mary Magdalene, who are said to have brought the Grail with them.

If either or both theories concerning Jesus's bloodline or his head were found to be true, the implications would be staggering. The authors of these speculative books are very much aware of the shocking nature of their findings, and that proof is needed to support their theories. They realize this means finding the Grail itself, be it an actual artefact or a scroll containing documentary evidence. Many of them, however, believe they are hot on the trail and that this discovery could be within reach.

Although the theories diverge, it is remarkable how many of them locate the Grail in the same place, namely Rosslyn Chapel, near Edinburgh. But to find out why this may be the final hiding-place of the Grail we must go back in time to when the Templars hurriedly escaped with their treasure, setting sail from La Rochelle on the west coast of France.

THE HIDDEN GRAIL

In 1307, twenty-four knights hurriedly set out in eighteen ships loaded with Templar treasures. Officially they disappeared, but it is known that at least one contingent arrived on the west coast of Scotland. There the Templars met up with their allies, the powerful St Clairs, whose family seat was at Roslin, near Edinburgh. At that time Scotland was independent of the Pope's jurisdiction due to the excommunication of Robert the Bruce, so it offered a safe home for the knights and their treasure. In this way, it is believed, the Grail passed into the keeping of the St Clair family. This idea seems to be confirmed by the fact that in 1446 William St Clair decided to build the curious and remarkable Rosslyn Chapel, known as the Chapel of the Grail.

APPLICATION - THE SECRET MESSAGE OF ROSSLYN

Rosslyn is a place of secrets. It puzzles and intrigues the Grail- seeker with its arcane symbolism and mystical atmosphere.

Nothing can replace the physical experience of being inside this astonishing building, but a visualization is offered for those who cannot make the journey.

VISULIZATION

As you approach this small chapel you notice how eccentric and heavy its architecture is. Coming closer you see it is flanked with an array of massive buttresses, which end at the facsimile of a ruined wall. The wall was copied from Solomon's Temple.

Entering the chapel you see at once that the stonework is covered with carvings. At first glance they appear to be Christian, but then you notice the face of a Green Man looking down from an archway, a horned devil peering from a pillar, a strange winged creature hanging upside down and bound by ropes. Above you the roof is a mass of decorations - daisies, lilies, roses and stars banded by sculpted arches. You look up at the rose window on the west wall and see that it is filled with an engrailed (scalloped) cross. This engrailed cross, which appears elsewhere, on shields and carvings, is the cross of the St Clairs. Walking around the chapel you notice a small but distinctive Templar tomb belonging to one of the many Williams of the St Clair family.

Looking towards the altar you see it is flanked by two great pillars. These represent the two great pillars of the Temple of Solomon, the priestly Jachin and the kinglyBoaz.Jachin is formed: of delicate columns interspersed with vertical- bands of ornate patterned carving. Boaz, by contrast has a large fluted central column spiraled round with bands of winding foliage.

According to a story connected with these two columns, after carving Jachin, the master mason went on holiday. While he was away his apprentice was inspired to carve the spiraling pillar, Boaz. However, when the master mason returned he was jealous of his apprentice's accomplishment and struck him such a blow that he killed him. Thereafter Boaz has always been referred to at theApprentice Pillar.It is now thought that this story was invented as a cover for an older story which is found in Freemasonry. It tells how Hiram Abif, a stonemason who worked on Solomon's Temple, was killed by a blow to the head because he would not divulge his secret knowledge to his apprentices.

Whether these stories are true or not, what is certain is that they demonstrate a link between the Holy Land, the Knights Templars and the Freemasons. In fact a close study of the stone carvings shows that pagan, Celtic and Masonic symbolism are all represented here. What the story also does is draw attention to the two pillars. However, the Mason's Pillar was plastered over for years to obscure the connection with Solomon's Temple, while the Apprentice Pillar has always been the focus of the chapel.

To the right of the Apprentice Pillar are steps going down to the crypt. It is dark and cold here with some strange drawings on the walls. It is said that at one time a figure of the Black Madonna was enshrined here. After a while you return to the chapel above. Looking around again you notice on the high altar a wooden cross with the head of Christ in the middle of it. There is so much to see and decipher, so many symbols and clues, that you almost feel overwhelmed. You realize you could spend hours here and still have new carvings to examine.

The Apprentice Pillar at Rosslyn Chapel

Returning finally to the Apprentice Pillar you notice a band of strange Nordic serpents coiled around its base. Could this pillar be symbolic of theYggdrasil,the World Tree of Norse mythology? You stand before it, seeking to penetrate its mysteries. Is the Holy Grail hidden within this pillar, as some believe, or does it lie beneath it? You know there are sealed vaults beneath the chapel that have never been excavated. Picture in your mind what you think they might reveal.

Chapter 10: The Grail Today

How blessed is Kabir, that amidst this great joy

   he sings within his own vessel.

It is the music of the meeting of soul with soul.

The nature of the Grail is to challenge settled views and present new ways of thinking. Down the centuries, as we have seen, it has always run counter to dogmatic belief. At the same time it seems to have had something of a love affair with established religion. It unsettles it, but is never far from it. A strongly feminine symbol, on both a spiritual and psychological level, the Grail has always offered an alternative spirituality with the potential to enrich more masculine forms of thinking and belief.

If we put together the Grail researchers' findings, both those on a physical and on a spiritual level, we can reach a greater appreciation of the Grail's potential. The Grail has always been strongly associated with the idea of blood, not only sacramentally, as in the blood of Christ, but also in terms of blood relations. The figure of Joseph of Arimathea has been used to suggest an alternative family of Grail guardians who are interrelated with the knights of Arthur - in particular, Perceval, Lancelot and Galahad. On a physical level this has led researchers to exciting and shocking possibilities, namely that Christ had children by the hitherto despised Mary Magdalene, and that these children were the forebears of European kings. On a spiritual one, it has taken us via the cult of the Magdalene into Gnosticism and the Feminine Mysteries.

As regards the other powerful physical and spiritual symbol, that of the severed head, it will be helpful to return to the oldest story of the Grail in existence, namelyPeredurin theMabtnogion.Unlike Chretien's unfinished story,Peredurdepicts the Grail as a severed head, and has an ending. This ending has often been ignored by scholars because it presents so many problems. Nevertheless, a reconsideration of it in the light of our researches, may yield some further insights.

TO THE ENDING OF THE GRAIL STORY

At first reading the ending of Peredur seems completely unsatisfactory. A yellow-hatred boy kneels before Peredur and admits to having been behind most of the female figures in the story, including the Black Woman and the Grail-bearer. He then says that the severed head belonged to Peredur's first cousin who was killed by the Hags of Gloucester, who also lamed his uncle. He ends by telling Peredur of the prophecy that he, Peredur, will take revenge. After this Peredur summons Arthur and his knights, who fight the hags and kill them after first giving them a chance to stop the fighting. The Hags consider themselves to be fated and keep fighting until eventually they are all killed.

THE YELLOW-HAIRED BOY

The first problem for the reader is that of the yellow-hatred boy claiming to be most of the women in the story. The scholar Roger Sherman Loomis has come up with a possible explanation for this. He argues that the old French word for 'high-born maiden' is damotsele, which differs from the word for 'high-born youth', damoisel, by only one letter, and could account for what seems like a confusion of masculine with feminine." If this were the case, then, instead of the youth, it would be a blonde-haired maiden who confessed to being both the Black Woman and Grail-bearer, This would accord with Celtic belief in the Maiden/Crone aspects of the Goddess and make the reading more satisfactory.

But even if we accept this as a reasonable explanation, there still remains the puzzle of the severed head and the Hags of Gloucester.

THE HAGS OF GLOUCESTER

All we know about the Hags of Gloucester is that there were nine of them and that they were warrior women with whom Peredur had previously trained for three weeks in the skills of horsemanship. The abilities of such women are well documented in Celtic myth. Many heroes, such as the Irish Cuchulain, were trained by women and it is not inappropriate for Peredur to have received lessons from them. On a symbolic level, however, the fact that they are described as hags suggests the figure of the Cailleach, whose warrior powers made her a type of challenger.

PRIESTESSES OF THE OTHERWORLD

In many of the Celtic and Arthurian tales the women are shown collectively, often in groups of nine. This could simply denote communities of women or, alternatively, it could represent the tripling of the triple-aspected goddess into a single great power. Whichever it is, the number is symbolic rather than actual and represents the feminine aspect in its fullest force.

In this respect correlations can be drawn between the various mystical groups of women in the legends. For example, the nine priestesses on theIslede Seinwho tend the souls of the dead must surely be linked with the nine priestesses who guard the magic cauldron of Annwn. Both groups of women are priestesses and both are linked to the Otherworld. The only difference is that one group tends the souls of the departed, while the other guards the magic cauldron. But are these different?

THE CASTLE OF MARVELS

At the end ofPeredurthe reader is directed to the Fortress of Marvels. In Chretien's story this is also called the Castle of Marvels and is inhabited by an imprisoned community of fatherless girls, disenfranchised widows and young men waiting to be knighted. Galahad breaks the spell and frees them all, knighting the young men. Then the story breaks off.

The Castle of Marvels is related to the Castle of Maidens who are also imprisoned and who are rescued by Galahad (see Chapter 7). This has been explained as an allegory in which Galahad, as a type of Christ, descends into Hell or the Otherworld and releases the imprisoned souls.

The idea of women representing the soul accords with psychological and esoteric thinking. Added to this, the various castles in the Arthurian legends have usually been viewed as types of the Otherworld. The Maidens of the Castle, therefore, are another type of collective femininity guarding the soul.

The Castle of Maidens was located near Gloucester. The nine Hags of Gloucester are connected with the Grail in the form of a severed head and they are fought by Arthur and his retinue. Therefore it may be that they are the dark counterparts of the nine priestesses who guard the Grail in Annwn, whom Arthur and his Knights also fight.

FEMININE VENGEANCE

If, as some scholars believe, there is a vengeance theme running through the stories of the Grail, this could lie in the conflict between the opposing energies of feminine and masculine principles. Whether or not the Hags of Gloucester represent the dark side of the feminine, they certainly oppose the masculine forces represented by Arthur and his knights. But at some level they know this creates imbalance and that they, in turn, are fated to be overcome.

THE SEVERED HEAD

The severed head forms part of the theme of feminine vengeance. In her dark aspect the feminine has severed the head of man and guards it. The head was regarded by the Celts as the seat of the soul. The dark feminine, therefore, guards the soul of man who is forced to brave her wrath in order to recover it. At the same time she acts as his challenger, deliberately provoking him into such action, knowing that her feminine energies need to be linked to male consciousness for full realization of their powers.

HEALING THE WASTE LAND

At present the land suffers greatly from the withdrawal of feminine understanding and nurturing. It has been raped by masculine greed and desire. The dishonored female hides and angrily withholds her wisdom. Yet she knows at some level that this is wrong. At the end of Wolfram'sParzival,Cundrie the Sorceress, who is treated with respect despite her hideousness, kneels before Perceval and asks him to pardon her. Then she assists both Perceval and his brother to achieve the Grail. After this there is great happiness and rejoicing, Perceval is reunited with his wife and Feirefiz marries the Grail maiden.

Perhaps it is no accident that Wolfram's text has recently gained such popularity. His version of the Grail story speaks, on many levels, of reconciliation. As such it is clearly relevant to us today. Any belief system which favors the masculine over the feminine, or the converse, risks continual feud, continual imbalance and sickness in the individual psyche as well as in the land. Both male and female need the 'freeing of the waters' for their survival. The earth has been dishonored and the land laid waste for too long. A truce must be called if human life is to continue. Male and female must learn to respect and honor each other's powers; they must also seek to balance their energies for the good of the earth.

Already, today, there are signs that this is beginning to happen. Male domination is being questioned and women are winning back respect and power. There is also a new awareness of the plight of the earth. At this most crucial time, it seems there is a real opportunity for healing and reconciliation at every level. This is the insight the Grail offers us today.

But the Grail never finishes with us. Even if this truce is achieved, it will demand more. The Grail is not only a symbol of balance and healing, it goes beyond reconciliation, calling mankind to the highest challenge of which it is capable. Ultimately, as Wolfram's text suggests, it requires nothing less than the mystical combustion and blending of feminine and masculine energies in its powerful matrix. Only in this way can the transformation of humanity, both psychologically and spiritually, finally be achieved.

APPLICATION - THE MYSTICAL EXPERIENCE

Any approach to the Grail must be made with the realization that its powers can be overwhelming. Its mystery is primarily experienced through the senses and it may be that you need to achieve it in stages. When using this visualization go only as far as you feel is appropriate.

Find a comfortable place and let your busy thoughts drop away, your mind go quiet. Imagine you are on a narrow path in a deep forest. Ahead of you is a pinpoint of light. As you approach you see it is a sanctuary. This may be a grove, a chapel, a tower, or a castle with a special room in it. As you get nearer you see it is filled with light, spilling out towards you. At the same time you become aware that you are surrounded by music' It is an outpouring of birdsong, rich and beautiful. Stop and listen to it.

When you are ready, move on towards your sanctuary. When you reach it, enter hesitantly, aware of its holiness. Ahead of you is a table and on the table a rich clothe. On the cloth is an object, which is difficult to see at first because it is sending out so much light.

Is it a chalice, a book, a beautiful carved stone or a jeweled crystal? As you approach, the light increases, a great fragrance fills the air and your senses are overwhelmed. Close your eyes.

Feel the light filling your head and running down your limbs. You are being washed through with light. Old' problems and difficulties, old fears and darkness's are being released as new energy pours in. Stay with this experience for as long as you can. Only if you are sure you are ready, touch or pick tip the object. Be careful because its power may be too strong for you at this time. If it is a stone or jewel, feel the concentration of its energy, look into its depths. What image do they contain? If it is a book, open it and see what it says. If it is a cup or chalice lift it to your lips. Let its healing draught flow into you, its healing powers work within you. Wait until you feel the work completed, until you are at peace.

Then slowly leave your inner sanctuary and come back into this world. Remember you can return there whenever you feel the need.

www.ingramcontent.com/pod-product-compliance
Lightning Source LLC
Chambersburg PA
CBHW050404120526
44590CB00015B/1816